A TALE OF TWO BRIDGES

A TALE OF
TWO BRIDGES

The San Francisco–Oakland Bay Bridges
of 1936 and 2013

Stephen D. Mikesell

UNIVERSITY OF NEVADA PRESS *Reno & Las Vegas*

University of Nevada Press, Reno, Nevada 89557 USA
www.unpress.nevada.edu
Copyright © 2017 by University of Nevada Press
Cover design by Martyn Schmoll
Cover photograph © Noah Clayton/Photodisc/Getty Images

LIBRARY OF CONGRESS CATALOGING-IN-PUBLICATION DATA
Names: Mikesell, Stephen D., author.
Title: A tale of two bridges : the San Francisco–Oakland Bay Bridges
    of 1936 and 2013 / Stephen D. Mikesell.
Description: Reno : University of Nevada Press [2016] | Includes
    bibliographical references and index.
Identifiers: LCCN 2016041579 (print) | LCCN 2016043725 (e-book) |
    ISBN 978-1-943859-26-9 (cloth : alkaline paper) |
    ISBN 978-0-87417-467-0 (e-book)
Subjects: LCSH: San Francisco–Oakland Bay Bridge (Oakland and
    San Francisco, Calif.)—History. | Suspension bridges—California—
    San Francisco Bay Area—Design and construction—History. |
    San Francisco (Calif.)—Buildings, structures, etc. | Oakland (Calif.)—
    Buildings, structures, etc.
Classification: LCC TG25.S237 M56 2016 (print) | LCC TG25.S237 (e-book) |
    DDC624.2/30979461—dc23 LC record available at
    https://lccn.loc.gov/2016041579

The paper used in this book meets the requirements of American
National Standard for Information Sciences—Permanence of Paper
for Printed Library Materials, ANSI/NISO z39.48-1992 (R2002).

FIRST PRINTING

Manufactured in the United States of America

Contents

Illustrations

Acknowledgments

This book reflects years of work researching historic bridges, especially those in California. I especially want to thank my colleagues at the California Department of Transportation (Caltrans), where I spent more than three years in the 1980s working on a comprehensive inventory of historic bridges in the state. That research led to a book, *Historic Highway Bridges of California* (1990), which featured photographs of the East Span and West Span on the San Francisco–Oakland Bay Bridge on the front and back covers. That research also led to historic bridge articles in *The Public Historian* and *The Southern California Quarterly*.

My work on the history of the Bay Bridge intensified in the 1990s, when I wrote the historical background section for Historic American Engineering Record documentation, in preparation for major modifications to the 1936 bridge. I want to thank my colleagues at JRP Historical Consulting for their support in this effort; I especially want to thank Monte Kim, who acted as my research assistant during this effort. The HAER report forms the basis for much of the chronology presented in chapters 1 through 6 of this book, although I have modified the discussion to reflect its larger analytical purposes.

I would also like to acknowledge the helpful criticism by readers of this work, especially the effort put in by Professor Michael Magliari of California State University–Chico. Finally, I want to recognize the many hours of editorial work put in by my wife, Suzanne Mikesell, a professional editor who did this work out of love.

A TALE OF TWO BRIDGES

Introduction

As this book was being written, two different eastern spans existed on Interstate 80 (I-80) between Yerba Buena Island and Oakland, California. One span was built in the mid-1930s but was taken out of service in 2013. The other span was built in 2013 and carries the busy traffic of I-80 to its western terminus in San Francisco. The California Department of Transportation (Caltrans), which owns both bridges, is dismantling the 1936 span. This book is a tale of these two bridges: the 1936 structure that opened to international acclaim and the 2013 structure, which was the subject of controversy and angst long before it opened on Memorial Day 2013.

The two spans have wildly different histories. When the old bridge opened in the 1930s, the Bay Area nearly shut down for four days of celebrations—parades on land, water, and in the air, speeches by federal and state officials, and a climactic telephone call from President Franklin Roosevelt to the toll gate operators (what a thrill for the operators!) to open the gates and let people use the bridge. When the second bridge opened in 2013, state, federal, and local officials largely shunned the ceremony. Even Governor Jerry Brown was away on vacation at the time and unable to attend. As the first cars traversed the roughly $7 billion span, engineers continued to debate the ultimate safety of the bridge.

The difference could hardly be more pronounced: The public almost universally acclaimed the old bridge as a great success. It openly derided the 2013 bridge as a costly failure. As one measure of the triumph of the 1936 span, the American Society of Civil Engineers in the mid-1950s included it in the most important engineering achievements in American history, dubbed the Seven

(*overleaf*) Two Bridges. Courtesy of the Jon B. Lovelace Collection of California Photographs in Carol M. Highsmith's America Project, Library of Congress, Prints and Photographs Division.

Wonders of the United States. It was joined by the Chicago sewer system, the Colorado River Aqueduct, the Empire State Building, the Grand Coulee Dam, the Hoover Dam, and the Panama Canal. This national recognition by the engineering community speaks to the degree to which the public revered the old bridge, more even than the immensely popular and nearby Golden Gate Bridge. By contrast, the national media has commonly referred to the 2013 span as a case study in how *not* to build a large public works project: it was a decade behind schedule, cost about seven times more than projections, and remains dogged by serious residual safety concerns.

A sizeable literature in the fields of engineering and planning has emerged analyzing megaprojects, defined as projects that involve complicated engineering challenges and cost more than $1 billion. The East Span of the Bay Bridge and the Big Dig in Boston have become the poster children for this body of work. The literature is so critical of both projects that it calls into question whether it is even possible under modern political conditions in the United States to carry off a megaproject without huge cost overruns and unconscionable delays.

Indeed, one of the best of the megaproject studies concerns the 2013 bridge, a study by Karen Trapenberg Frick titled "The Making and Un-Making of the San Francisco–Oakland Bay Bridge."[1] Among its many outstanding attributes, Frick's study invents the six C's model for defining a megaproject: colossal, costly, captivating, controversial, complex, and control. Frick argues that the 2013 replacement structure was alluring to decision-makers because it was colossal and captivating. The engineers at Caltrans in particular were captivated by the idea of designing and building a huge new structure and were far less captivated by the prospect of repairing the 1936 bridge that had been damaged in the 1989 Loma Prieta earthquake. The other four C's, however, undid these engineering plans: the replacement span cost way beyond anyone's worst nightmare, resulting in a huge public and governmental controversy. Also, Caltrans and Bay Area transportation planners found that the task of managing both political and technical people proved too complex. Ultimately, the whole project spun out of control.

This book is a history of the two bridges. The essential question I pose in this book is, Why was the 1936 bridge so successful and the 2013 bridge so unsuccessful? The corollary questions are, What did people do right in 1936? What did they do wrong in 2013?

In fairness to those responsible for the 2013 bridge, the conditions under which engineers and contractors built the 1936 bridge were exactly suited to a heroic engineering feat like the Bay Bridge. The public and decision-makers believed that the bridge was necessary from a transportation standpoint. The country was in economic collapse, making large, job-creating public works projects hugely popular. The project was so universally supported by local, state, and federal officials that those leaders gave California's Department of Public Works free rein in planning and building the bridge.

That free rein, however, would have been withdrawn quickly had the bridge been delayed for a decade, experienced seven-fold cost overruns, or developed worrisome safety concerns, the mistakes that marred the 2013 span. The fact is the 1936 bridge was constructed on time and slightly under budget. At the same time, it conquered huge and unprecedented engineering challenges, using materials and construction techniques deemed crude by modern standards. The people who built the 1936 bridge accomplished something very special in the history of what are now called *megaprojects*. The contrast between the experiences in 1936 and 2013 is remarkable—not so much because of the failures of 2013, but because the 1936 success was so pronounced and complete. Comparing the two experiences is worthwhile not for the purpose of criticizing modern planners, but to gain an understanding of how and why the 1936 planners were able to accomplish so much.

This book will explore the transportation needs the 1936 bridge was designed to address. It will also detail the decades of controversy and inertia that delayed construction of the bridge, which provides a hint of why more-recent megaprojects often fail. It will delve into the specifics of the design and construction of the 1936 bridge, explore the administrative and technical structure used, and suggest a model for how to plan megaprojects in the future.

Finally, the book will examine how and why things went awry in 2013 and contrast the reasons for that failure with the contrasting experience that culminated in the much more successful effort in 1936. We might be tempted to throw up our hands and conclude, as did the authors of a recent study of Boston's Big Dig, that fragmentation of the modern political process combined with onerous environmental constraints make it virtually impossible to build a megaproject with the efficiency of the huge projects of the 1930s.[2] With the 2013 bridge project, we can identify the specific errors that ensured the project would be terribly late, over budget, and vulnerable to safety concerns. While the modern political process is undeniably more complex than that of New Deal California, individuals and individual decisions led to the problems of the 2013 span. And examining those people and decisions in light of the equivalent decisions made by the designers of the 1936 span can lead to better outcomes in the future.

Through it all, this book is a tribute to the Bay Bridge, in service for nearly eighty years; it has greatly transformed life in the Bay Area, and in Oakland and San Francisco in particular. Although often overlooked in our adoration of the nearby Golden Gate Bridge, it is the Bay Bridge that makes things work in the Bay Area and without which the prosperity of the modern Bay Area would not be possible.

Notes

1. Karen Trapenberg Frick, "The Making and Un-Making of the San Francisco–Oakland Bay Bridge: A Case in Megaproject Planning and Decisionmaking" (doctoral dissertation, University of California–Berkeley, Fall 2005). This doctoral dissertation was revised and published as Frick, *Remaking the San Francisco–Oakland Bay Bridge: A Case of Shadowboxing with Nature* (London: Routledge, 2015).

2. Alan Altshuler and David Luberoff, *Mega-Projects: The Changing Politics of Urban Public Investment* (Washington, DC: Brookings Institution, 2003). The Altshuler and Luberoff study will be examined in great detail in the conclusion of this book.

CHAPTER 1

Transportation in the Bay Area Before the Bay Bridge

Historians generally agree that the Bay Bridge revolutionized transportation in the Bay Area and throughout Northern California, without specifying the transportation modes it affected. This chapter attempts to measure that impact with reference to the three principal means of travel impacted by construction of this bridge: navigation, mass transit, and vehicular traffic.

Like most great urban areas in the United States, the San Francisco Bay Area was settled first by sea; it was only later linked to the rest of California and the nation through ground transportation modes. Historian Kevin Starr observed, "No American city is more fortunately, or more unfortunately, sited than San Francisco, surrounded by water on three sides. San Francisco stands in splendid isolation, a virtual island off the coast."[1] The East Bay and Peninsula cities were also settled initially via sea but were more quickly provided with effective ground transportation than was San Francisco. Among its many contributions to the settlement history of the Bay Area, the Bay Bridge for the first time provided San Francisco with a direct ground link to the East Bay and thus to the rest of America.

Navigation in the Bay Area before the Bay Bridge

Navigation in the Bay Area before the building of the Bay Bridge can be seen as comprising two basic modes: cargo-carrying ships that plied the oceans and inland waters, and ferries that carried passengers and sometimes their automobiles around the Bay Area and occasionally as far as Sacramento. These two modes had different hubs at different times.

In terms of oceangoing freight, San Francisco was, from the 1850s through the 1930s, one of the great port cities of the world. By the time the Bay Bridge was built, however, the dominance of the Port of San Francisco was beginning to erode; by the 1960s Oakland was the clear leader in port activities, chiefly because Oakland was linked to good rail and truck routes while San Francisco was not. Port development in Oakland was hampered throughout the nineteenth century by uncertain ownership of land at the waterfront. An 1892 U.S. Supreme Court decision confirmed that most of the waterfront was owned by the city of Oakland, a decision that removed the last major impediment to development there. The Oakland Harbor was expanded during American involvement in World War I. Then, in 1927, the city of Oakland created a separate port department (now the Board of Port Commissioners) and the modern Port of Oakland was created.[2]

During the decade between 1921 and 1931, the ports in Oakland and San Francisco both experienced explosive growth in commercial shipping, although the pace of growth favored Oakland. Prior to 1927 (when the Port of Oakland was formally organized), shipping tonnage in San Francisco more than doubled that in Oakland. By 1921 the gap had narrowed: Oakland handled about three-quarters the tonnage of San Francisco. Oakland's port would continue to outgrow San Francisco's through World War II before overwhelming it during the 1950s and 1960s.

The Bay Bridge did not directly affect the decline of shipping in San Francisco or its ascension in Oakland; that trend is best attributed to improvements in freight rail connections in Oakland and the emergence of land-intensive transshipment methods, both of which worked against the pinched-in port in San Francisco. As discussed later, however, the Bay Bridge did revolutionize trucking in the Bay Area, which was one major part of the transformation of cargo handling. Any oceangoing shipment that was partially intended for San Francisco, for example, could, after construction of the Bay Bridge, be easily transported to the city of San Francisco by truck from Oakland, something that was impossible before the bridge.

Another important part of shipping in the Bay Area before and just after the Bay Bridge was built was the use of the region by the military. It is difficult today to imagine the Bay Area in 1930, when it was one of the most important military hubs in the United

Aerial view of San Francisco Bay, before construction of Bay Bridge, 1934. Courtesy of Library of Congress. LC-USZ62-127221 (b&w film copy neg.)

States. Following the end of the Cold War, the military has nearly abandoned the Bay Area, leaving only small pockets of high-tech activity still in place. In 1930, however, the region was filled with big and important bases. The Army was well represented with its Presidio of San Francisco (the headquarters to the Fourth Army and home to thousands of soldiers), as well as Fort Mason, and (later) the Oakland Army Base, both important quartermaster facilities. It was the Navy, however, that had a huge presence in the Bay Area around the time of construction of the Bay Bridge, including a large station on Yerba Buena Island (to be joined in the later 1930s by an even larger station on man-made Treasure Island), huge air stations in Sunnyvale and Alameda, major ship construction and repair facilities at Mare Island in Vallejo and at Hunters Point in San Francisco, a supply station in Oakland and another near Stockton, and miscellaneous smaller facilities scattered throughout the Bay Area.

In the 1920s it was not at all clear that San Diego was going to win its long contest with San Francisco for supremacy in naval matters. In the late 1920s San Diego and San Francisco and, to a lesser degree, Los Angeles, vied to be the center of U.S. Navy activities on the Pacific coast. The Navy for its part was content to let the competition go forward, exacting increasingly generous concessions from the host communities.[3] The outcome remained uncertain while the Bay Bridge was being planned, a fact that actually delayed construction of the bridge.

With so many active and proposed military bases around the Bay, the War Department jealously protected sea lanes for Navy and Army ships as well as port facilities on the East Bay and in San Francisco, some of which it eyed as potential military bases. The War Department objections were the principal reasons why local interests were unable to build a bridge during the 1920s, when Bay Area interests studied the project in great detail. It was not until the intervention of President Herbert Hoover in the early 1930s that the region and the state overcame these War Department objections.

A third important element of navigation prior to construction of the Bay Bridge was the development of a comprehensive and integrated system of passenger and vehicular ferries. In retrospect, we can see that these private ferries did for the Bay Area in the 1920s what would have been accomplished more cheaply and more effectively by the Bay Bridge, had it been built during that decade. As discussed later, there was an exploding suburbanization of the Bay Area population during the 1920s, facilitated by growth of interurban trolleys and highway-based automobile and truck traffic. The interurban and highway systems were quite efficient for their time in every respect except one: they could not go directly across San Francisco Bay. In time, this barrier would be conquered by the Bay Bridge. During the 1920s, however, the best solution available was to carry these hundreds of thousands of passengers and automobiles across the Bay by ferry boat.

As part of early state planning for the Bay Bridge in 1929–30, the California Division of Highways conducted an exhaustive study of passenger and vehicular ferry use in the Bay Area between 1915 and 1929. There were two compelling reasons to complete this study. First, the extensive use of ferries, particularly

Ferry Building at evening. Courtesy of Library of Congress. LC-USZ62-137812 (b&w film copy neg.)

vehicular ferries, provided a justification for building the bridge, what transportation planners today call the "purpose and need" for the project. Second, and perhaps even more important, the state saw ferry fees as a rough estimate for the income it could count on to repay construction loans for the bridge. In short, the transfer of ferry fees to bridge tolls was seen as a possible, perhaps even primary, source of revenue to repay loans for the bridge.[4]

The raw numbers and trends in ferry use clearly supported the purpose and need for the bridge. The unmistakable trend between 1915 and 1929 was a decline in passenger-only ferry use and a huge increase in automobile ferry use. Passenger-only use was linked to the interurban trolley system; in other words, the passengers arrived at the ferry site via an interurban. This use, while very large throughout the period, declined 10 percent over the fourteen years of the study, from 38.75 million passengers in 1915 to 35.92 million passengers in 1929. Vehicular ferry service followed a much different trajectory. In 1915 1.75 million passengers rode the ferries with their cars. In 1929 that number was 10.17 million, an increase of more than 600 percent. By 1929 passenger-only ferry use still outnumbered vehicular ferry use by about three to one, but that gap was closing quickly.

The growth in vehicular ferry use, of course, correlated directly with the increasing automobile registration and the development of good highways, discussed later under the chapter on highway transportation. It might also be explained by improved levels of service during the 1920s, as the Golden Gate Ferry line came to dominate vehicle ferry service in much the same way that its parent corporation, the Southern Pacific Railroad, dominated freight and passenger rail service. Prior to World War I ferries would accept automobiles only as space permitted. In 1920 however, Aven Hanford organized the Golden Gate Ferry line, with the specific mission of providing transport for automobiles. The line initially ran between Sausalito and San Francisco but quickly spread to connect San Francisco to various locations in Marin, Alameda, and Contra Costa Counties. The Southern Pacific Railroad had ventured into automobile ferry service on its own but in 1929 bought out the Golden Gate Ferry line operation, achieving a near monopoly on this service.[5]

Although the Bay Bridge had no specific navigational function, navigational issues would dominate debate about the bridge throughout the 1920s and into the 1930s. Most discussions focused on the need to avoid blocking access to the emerging Port of Oakland. The need to preserve shipping lanes to Oakland and to nearby military bases led to some of the most dramatic engineering challenges in designing the bridge.

The single most dramatic and direct effect of building the Bay Bridge was the crippling of ferry service between the East Bay and San Francisco. This service was alive and profitable before the bridge was built, but virtually disappeared after 1936, not to be revived for more than half a century.

Mass Transit Interurban Rail Service before the Bay Bridge

At the time the Bay Bridge was built, commuter rail lines in most of the United States were called *interurban rail lines*, or simply *interurbans*. The term referred to a function rather than a type of rail car. The interurban system of the Bay Area at the time was the functional equivalent of the modern Bay Area Rapid Transit (BART) rather than, say, the San Francisco Municipal Railway (Muni). The interurbans, as the name implies, connected different urban areas, much as BART today connects disparate communities in several Bay Area counties.

Mass transit developed differently in San Francisco than elsewhere in the Bay Area. The street railway system in San Francisco was intra-urban: it was designed to move people within that city, with limited connectivity with systems outside the city of San Francisco. The trolleys and cable cars existed to serve the people of San Francisco. By 1930 most of the mass transit network in San Francisco was municipally owned; only the Market Street Railway remained in private hands. Ridership on the San Francisco railways peaked in the mid-1930s but declined rapidly during the remainder of that decade.[6]

East Bay interurbans, by contrast, were privately owned at the time the Bay Bridge was built and existed primarily to move workers to and from the East Bay suburbs and San Francisco. The interurban system had always operated in conjunction with privately owned ferry lines, with each rail line owning its own ferries. In a sense, it is a somewhat artificial distinction between navigational aspects of the ferry system and the mass transit aspects of the interurbans: the two were simply different modes within an integrated network.

The concept of an integrated rail-ferry service began with the Central (later Southern) Pacific Railroad in the nineteenth century. The Southern Pacific had provided some type of passenger rail service in the East Bay since the 1860s and began integrated interurban and ferry service from the Oakland Mole in the 1880s.[7] Its system was electrified in 1911 and provided passenger interurban-ferry connections via the Oakland Mole as well as a mole on Alameda Island. At the time of its electrification, the Southern Pacific's interurban lines from the Oakland Mole included two Oakland lines, two Berkeley lines, and a San Leandro line; there were two lines in Alameda leading to the Alameda Mole.[8]

Although the Southern Pacific was first to provide service, it was the Key System that came to dominate interurban service by the time the Bay Bridge was built in the mid-1930s. The Key System was assembled by Francis Marion Smith, often called "Borax" Smith, and one of the more interesting entrepreneurs in California history. Born in Wisconsin in 1846, Smith left for the American West at the age of twenty-one. He and his brother began mining borax in Nevada in the early 1870s. He established a huge borax empire in the Death Valley region of California and eventually owned mining properties throughout the world. In the

1920s he expanded his empire to include real estate development in the San Francisco Bay Area and his Key System was initially developed to offer interurban access to his East Bay real estate holdings.[9]

Smith and his partners and successors assembled the Key System from existing steam lines as well as through new construction. Most of the system had been electrified by the turn of the twentieth century. Like the Southern Pacific, the Key System maintained its own fleet of ferries. The Key System ferries docked at the grand Key System Mole, which was immediately south of the future locations of the toll booth and Oakland touchdown for the Bay Bridge. The Key System Mole reached farther and farther into the bay over time. At the time the Bay Bridge was built, the Key System Mole extended nearly halfway between the Oakland–Emeryville shoreline and Yerba Buena Island. The elegant ferry terminal structure at the end of the mole was destroyed in a massive explosion in 1933, while the Bay Bridge was under construction. The ferry house was rebuilt with mundane steel buildings.

By the late 1920s there were eight major Key System lines, extending to Piedmont, Claremont, Berkeley, and various parts of Oakland. The system also included light trolley service that fed into the heavier interurban lines.

As noted, Smith built the Key System chiefly to provide access to land he owned and wanted to subdivide. In 1927 Smith and his Key System partners filed for bankruptcy for the Key System but held on to their far more profitable real estate operation. San Francisco banking interests, led by Alfred Lundberg, reorganized the Key System and operated under that name until abandoning the system in the 1950s.[10]

The popularity of the interurban commute and associated real estate development worked together to develop a settlement pattern that, somewhat ironically, would be used to justify construction of the predominantly automobile-oriented Bay Bridge. The interurbans had facilitated population growth in the East Bay and that population growth in turn resulted in population densities that were capable of supporting the rail operations. In time, the state of California would use the impressive ridership

Key System Mole and Bay Bridge. Courtesy of San Francisco History Center, San Francisco Public Library.

on the interurbans and ferries as a basis for building the bridge. The state argued that there were tens of thousands of commuters willing to pay a substantial fare to take a relatively slow commute via train and ferry to San Francisco. The state opined (correctly) that many of those commuters would be willing to take a faster interurban ride when the rails were extended to San Francisco on the bridge, or the even faster commute via automobile across the bridge. The proposed bridge, they argued, could deliver all of those commuters to San Francisco more cheaply and quickly than the Key System or its competitors, and the state was absolutely correct in that regard.

In 1929–30 state transportation planners prepared an exhaustive study of where commuters to San Francisco lived, as an initial step in the locational studies for the bridge.[11] The state's studies portrayed an interurban-ferry traffic that was vigorous but showing signs of decay. Those data showed that East Bay to San Francisco traffic was extraordinarily high in 1915, a figure skewed by the powerful draw of the World's Fair held in the city that year. Traffic decreased dramatically in 1916, then rose steadily between 1917 and 1925. Between 1925 and 1929 (the last year data were available for the study), there was a steady decline in traffic on all lines under study: the Key System at the Key System Mole, the Southern Pacific line at the Oakland Mole, and the Alameda line at the Alameda Mole.

The state's consultant, Lester Ready, also studied automobile-ferry traffic going into San Francisco, a logical choice because he was planning for a bridge that would accommodate rail as well as automobile commuters. Ready distributed more than 24,000 questionnaire cards to interurban-ferry customers and 10,000 cards to automobile-ferry users, seeking to determine where the commuters lived and where they worked, again, to determine the most effective location for the new bridge. The cards were passed out between 4:00 PM and 6:00 PM, targeting the commuters for whom the bridge was being built.

Ready divided the Bay Area into ninety-eight zones: forty-nine in San Francisco and forty-nine outside the city. Ready's data showed several unmistakable trends. First, the points of origin for interurban commuters were East Bay communities well served by the Key System, with Berkeley, Oakland, and Alameda leading the group. Second, the automobile commuters originated in communities that were not well served by the Key System but that had good highways. These included outlying areas of Oakland and Berkeley, and more-distant communities such as Richmond and small towns south of Oakland.

The ultimate result of Ready's study was to pin down the best location for the Bay Bridge. From time to time, various transportation planners had suggested various alignments other than the one eventually chosen, with a southern crossing from Alameda to Hunters Point being the most popular alternative. Ready's data, however, showed that the alignment running from the Key System Mole to Mission Street in San Francisco was the best location from nearly every standpoint. It landed in the San Francisco business district, where most of the commuters worked. It followed the exact alignment of the Key System, a route already being taken daily by tens of thousands of commuters. The bridge, by carrying the actual Key System cars across the bay, would do everything the ferries would do but would cut ten minutes from the bay crossing. It also linked well with the highway system in the East Bay and would deliver automobile commuters to their places of work while cutting an expected half-hour from the commute in each direction.

By the time the Bay Bridge was built in the mid-1930s, the interurbans were recognized as an important, although declining, factor in the integrated transportation network of the Bay Area. A solution to traffic problems in the Bay Area would necessarily take the interurbans into account. These trolleys were essential parts of the current system and were seen as key to the future as well. That alone explains why rails were built into the Bay Bridge.

Highway Transportation Before the Bay Bridge Was Built

Of the major modes of transportation in the Bay Area, highways remained the least developed at the time the Bay Bridge was authorized. The highway system of the Bay Area, and California generally, would be revolutionized in the post–World War II era, when the number of highways and highway lanes increased dramatically. By comparison with the levels of development in navigation and interurban rail lines, the highway system in the Bay Area was still in its infancy in 1930.

Nonetheless, the highway network of the Bay Area had matured since the early 1920s, owing chiefly to the construction of major state highways. The California State Highway System dates to 1896, when the first road—an abandoned toll road between Placerville and Lake Tahoe—was taken over by the state.[12] The institutional arrangement for state highway construction and maintenance evolved slowly over the following decades. In 1907 the state legislature created the California Department of Engineering, empowering it to build new highways on the basis of annual appropriations by the legislature. A major step forward was passage of a bond measure in 1909, giving the Department of Engineering a more secure source of funding. Better and more-dependable funding was provided by vehicle registration fees, which were initiated in 1914. Voters passed additional highway construction bond measures in 1916 and 1919. The most significant step in securing dependable funds for building highways came in 1923, when the state for the first time enacted a gasoline tax, earmarking half of all funds for state highway construction and the other half for local roads.[13] The gasoline tax was increased by 50 percent in 1927, with all of the increase dedicated to building and maintaining state highways.

The 1923 and 1927 gasoline taxes ushered in one of the most prodigious periods of highway construction in California history, rivaling the early freeway construction era of the early 1950s. The tax revenues reserved for building state highways brought in funds at a rate that was sufficient to finance highway projects in all parts of the state. Meanwhile, federal aid for highway construction, initiated in 1916, also grew at an accelerated pace during the 1920s.

The growth in the number of highways built in California during the 1920s was much higher than the national average, as was automobile registration and use, but the state was not alone in this regard. Historians have credited a range of automobile-related developments—from building roads to suburban housing tracts—for fueling the prosperity of that decade in American economic history. As Thomas Cochran observed, "No one has or perhaps can reliably estimate the vast size of capital invested in reshaping society to fit the automobile.... The total capital investment was probably the major factor in the boom of the 1920s, and hence the glorification of American business."[14]

The Bay Area was the most densely settled region of California in 1920 and garnered its share of state highway construction funds during this period. Virtually every modern highway in the Bay Area was either initiated or improved during the 1920s. The situation can be illustrated with reference to four of the most important highways in the region: U.S. 101 along the Peninsula, following the alignment of the modern Bayshore Freeway; the East Bay State Highway, essentially the alignment of modern interstate 880 (I-880); the road from Vallejo to Oakland, the equivalent of the modern I-80 corridor; and the road from the San Ramon Valley to Oakland, the equivalent of modern State Route 24.

Until the 1920s the main roadway from San Jose to San Francisco was the El Camino Real, roughly the alignment of the historic Spanish Royal Road linking the missions in Santa Clara and

San Francisco, and denoted today by State Route 82. The state of California recognized the importance of this route early in the twentieth century. Contract No. 1, the first to be let using funds from the 1909 bond act, provided for the paving of this route. Many small communities along this road would become larger communities. By the end of the 1920s the El Camino in Santa Clara, San Mateo, and San Francisco Counties was the most congested road in the state highway system.[15]

Throughout the 1920s civic and political leaders in those counties lobbied for a two-pronged solution to traffic congestion: widening the El Camino, and building an entirely new highway along the edge of San Francisco Bay, following the route now taken by the Bayshore Freeway. The El Camino was widened as a stopgap measure, going from twenty feet to fifty feet, or in some cases a hundred feet, during this decade.[16]

The more significant development, however, was construction of an entirely new highway along the Bay. The design criteria for this new thoroughfare was described in detail by Col. John Skeggs, who served as the district engineer for the local offices of the division of highways during the time the Bayshore was built: "The answer to the imperious demands of the traffic was soon discovered by civic leaders and engineers of the city and state, and consisted of two parts: first, the widening and improvement of El Camino Real, which was undertaken forthwith; second: a new, broad highway from near the center of the city [San Francisco] to San Jose, located as far east as practicable, of the existing highways and the towns, strung like beads along it."[17]

The Bayshore Highway (as it was called until renamed the Bayshore Freeway in the 1950s) was still under construction in 1930. The first sixteen miles, completed in 1929 between San Francisco and the town of San Mateo, was a stunning piece of roadway engineering for its time, as noted by District Engineer Skeggs: "This work, in both instances [inside and outside San Francisco] involved construction of the heaviest character and on a scale never before undertaken by either the city or the state."[18] The paved surface was 100 feet wide inside a right-of-way that stretched 125 feet. This massive road (at least in the context of road building in the 1920s) was essentially a proto-freeway that

Bayshore Highway. Courtesy of San Francisco History Center, San Francisco Public Library.

could easily be adapted for later designation as a freeway. When the initial segment of the Bayshore Highway was upgraded to freeway status in 1947, it became the first freeway in the Bay Area.[19]

The division pursued a parallel development in the East Bay, although construction there lagged behind that on the Peninsula. Skeggs observed this parallel in noting that the state highway between Oakland and San Jose "has gradually assumed the importance to Oakland, San Jose, and east bay territory which the Peninsula Highway bears to San Francisco, San Jose, and peninsula territory."[20] In 1915 the Oakland–San Jose road was built and paved to eighteen feet within a twenty-four feet right-of-way. Throughout the 1920s the division of highways rebuilt and expanded portions of this roadway, with each new section wider than the last. The first sections were widened to a thirty-foot paved surface. Sections built in 1928 included a sixty-foot paved surface within a hundred-foot right-of-way. Although not as wide as the Bayshore, the East Bay Highway was also a freeway in the making, a gigantic roadway in the context of the times. The subsequent Eastshore Freeway, completed in the 1950s, easily reused much of what had been built in the 1920s.[21]

This work on both sides of the Bay was under way at the time the Bay Bridge was approved; much of it was under construction while the Bay Bridge was being built. The district engineer noted the relationship between these two proto-freeways and the proposed Bay Bridge. Writing in 1930 he observed, "This section of highway [the East Bay Highway] holds a particularly important position with respect to east bay communities due to the excellently paved connections at many points leading to both the transbay bridges. Northbound traffic is afforded quick access to San Francisco via the San Francisco Bay bridge and the Bayshore Highway. Southbound traffic enjoys equally good connections with the Dumbarton Bridge leading to Palo Alto and adjacent peninsula territory."[22]

In addition, the division of highways during the 1920s was designing and starting construction of a northern extension of the East Bay Highway, designed to bypass a highly congested state highway that followed what is now San Pablo Avenue through Oakland, Emeryville, and Berkeley. Like the Bayshore Freeway on the Peninsula, the East Bay Highway north of Oakland was built on an entirely new alignment that hugged the Bay, to the point that much of it was built on fill. This highway was not completed by the opening of the Bay Bridge, a fortuitous fact in that it allowed the division of highways to construct simultaneously the bridge and the most substantial roadway leading to it. The division built a complex distribution structure resembling a modern freeway interchange that connected the north–south oriented East Bay Freeway to the bridge, as well as older east–west roadways in Oakland.

The Vallejo-to-Oakland road, now part of I-80 (as is the Bay Bridge), was a minor road until the 1920s, when construction of the Carquinez Bridge made this the preferred connector between the Bay Area and points east, including Sacramento. The Carquinez Bridge revolutionized traffic patterns between Sacramento and the Bay Area. Completed in 1927 by the American Toll Bridge Company, the span ensured that transcontinental traffic as well as more localized traffic would be routed from the Central Valley through Vallejo and the East Bay, as opposed to the Altamont Pass and other alternative alignments.

The Carquinez Bridge was completed about the time that debates over the Bay Bridge entered a critical phase. Although the Carquinez Bridge could accommodate reasonably heavy traffic, the bridge was grafted onto a system of inadequate highways on either side of the Carquinez Strait. If this private toll bridge was to fulfill its promise, the connecting roadways would need to be improved. Fortunately, this work was already under way and would be finished just in time to feed traffic to the completed Bay Bridge.

Like the East Bay and Bayshore Highways, a new road from the Carquinez Bridge at Vallejo to Sacramento was planned as an entirely new alignment, separated from the old U.S. 40 (the most popular of various versions of the Lincoln Highway) as much as possible. As the district engineer observed in 1936, "Considerable thought was given to a direct road that would be away from the present road for almost its entire distance."[23]

This new alignment, which followed closely the modern I-80 route, was only partially completed by the time the Bay Bridge opened. The division of highways, which was stretched thin from a huge number of construction projects statewide in the mid-1930s, concentrated on the worst bottlenecks. It completed the Cordelia Bypass in 1929, a 1.2 mile stretch of new road west of Fairfield. In the early 1930s it completed two additional bypasses, including a long and expensive route around Vacaville and the even more expensive American Canyon Cut-Off, which bypassed Vallejo. The American Canyon Cut-Off included six miles of new road that took "traffic off a considerable length of narrow, crooked streets in the City of Vallejo, and eliminated five grade crossings with railroads." Taken together with changes on the same alignment between the Carquinez Bridge and Oakland, these improvements shaved an hour off the driving time between Sacramento and the Oakland approach to the Bay Bridge, making it "an easy two-hour trip at the present speed limit between Sacramento and San Francisco."[24]

Meanwhile, the route from the San Ramon Valley to Oakland further illustrates the prodigious rate of highway construction that took place during the decade before the Bay Bridge was built, as well as the uncertainties about how such highway work could be financed. The mountain range that separates the East Bay from the San Ramon Valley forced traffic between these two areas to detour dozens of miles through Richmond to the north or the South Bay to the south.[25] The situation improved marginally in 1903 when Alameda County built the Broadway Tunnel, high on the hillside between the two communities. This 1,040-foot long wood-lined tunnel was useful for some purposes but was generally too small for trucks and too slow for commuters.

Motorists pleaded for an improved tunnel but work was stalled for a variety of reasons, not the least of which was the fact that the proposed tunnel began and ended in different counties. This jurisdictional problem was ultimately solved through creation of a Joint Highway District, which allowed Alameda and Contra Costa Counties to pool resources and income to build a shared facility. The tunnel, ultimately called the Caldecott Tunnel, was approved in 1929 but not completed until 1937, about a year after completion of the Bay Bridge. A major share of the construction cost was provided by the federal Public Works Administration, a New Deal agency. Although designed and built through the cooperation of local government, the Caldecott Tunnel and connecting roads served regional traffic needs and were ultimately incorporated into the state highway system.[26]

These four major highways were the most important but by no means the only highways to be built or rebuilt in California during the 1920s. There were two closely related developments that drove economic growth in the Golden State during the 1920s: a huge jump in automobile ownership and a corresponding increase in highway construction. For whatever reasons, Californians were quicker than other Americans to adopt the automobile as the mainstay for business and pleasure travel. In 1929 Californians owned one car for every 2.7 people. In the Northeast, that figure was 5.6, in the South it was 7.1, and in the other western states it was 4.0.[27] With so many automobiles around and generating bountiful gasoline tax revenues, it was logical to expect that the state would build roads to service those many vehicles. The division of highways did not merely spend money on roads: it did so wisely and with an eye toward bypassing the worst traffic bottlenecks.

It was not accidental that the most important new highways from the 1920s converged near the eastern and western approaches of what would become the Bay Bridge. As discussed, the planners for the Bay Bridge did due diligence research on how best to locate the bridge to maximize its utility and fare-generating capacity. They selected a spot that lay at a critical juncture for the East Bay Highway, the Vallejo Road, and the Caldecott Tunnel Road in the East Bay and at the terminus of the Bayshore Freeway on the west side.

To some degree the situation with cars and trucks was analogous to that for interurban trains in 1929. There was a usable highway system on both sides of the Bay in 1929, just as there were usable mass transit systems on each side of the Bay. The problem was that the two systems, East Bay and West Bay, could not directly connect with one another. That, ultimately, was why the Bay Bridge was built, to end a dependence on intervening Bay ferries to directly link the efficient and growing highway and transit systems on two sides of the Bay. It was multimodal from the outset because it was overtly designed to assist in linking two different types of travel that flourished on both sides of the Bay.

Unfortunately, the designers of the Bay Bridge were better at structural engineering than traffic forecasting. As the Bay Bridge opened in 1936, Earl Lee Kelly, the director of Public Works for the state of California, proudly proclaimed that the bridge would accommodate all current and future traffic needs of the region and that traffic would be split among cars and trolleys. By 1950, he predicted, the bridge would carry about 78 million people between Oakland and San Francisco each year, with 16 percent going by automobile, 32 percent by bus, and 51 percent by train. He predicted the bridge could accommodate this level of service "without congestion" through the year 1975.[28]

Kelly and the others who built the bridge understood that automobile traffic was growing faster than mass transit use but they also saw a healthy, if not altogether robust, mass transit ridership. They could not have foreseen that by 1975 the number of people crossing the bridge would be double the figure they predicted, and that the percentage of people carried by train would not be 51 percent but 0 percent. And, of course, they could not have foreseen that traffic would not be "without congestion" but rather would be maddeningly congested, beyond Earl Lee Kelly's worst nightmare.

What Kelly and the others failed to appreciate was the depth of commitment to automobile-only commuting shared by Bay Area residents, a commitment that only deepened when the Bay Bridge shaved a half-hour each way from the East Bay to San Francisco auto commute. Kelly and the others assumed that the mix of commuting by car, bus, and trolley would remain the same when the bridge was built. It did not, and the massive shift to the automobile that resulted became the major contribution of the Bay Bridge to transportation development in the Bay Area. Transportation patterns were not altered—they were revolutionized.

Notes

1. Kevin Starr, *Endangered Dreams: The Great Depression in California* (New York: Oxford University Press, 1996), 324.

2. The history of the Port of Oakland is detailed in a 1977 edition of *Port-Progress*, a journal of the Port, entitled, "125 Years of Waterfront Growth, as Compiled on the 50th Anniversary of the Oakland Board of Port Commissioners, 1927–1977."

3. This inter-city competition for military bases is a central point in Roger W. Lotchin, *Fortress California: From Warfare to Welfare, 1910–1960* (New York: Oxford University Press, 1992).

4. This study of ferry traffic was contained in the Hoover–Young San Francisco Bay Bridge Commission, "Report to the President of the United States and the Governor of California," August 1930, hereafter cited as *Hoover-Young Commission Report.*

5. See George H. Harlan, *San Francisco Bay Ferryboats* (Berkeley, CA: Howell-North Books, 1967).

6. See Paul C. Trimble, *Railways of San Francisco* (Charleston, SC: Arcadia Books, 2004).

7. The Oakland Mole was a later name for the Oakland Long Wharf, an earthen berm at the foot of Seventh Street, in the Port of Oakland. It was some distance south of the Key System Mole, discussed later.

8. Paul C. Trimble, *Interurban Railways of the Bay Area* (Fresno, CA: Valley Publishers, 1977). See also Paul C. Trimble and John C. Alioto Jr., *The Bay Bridge* (Charleston, SC: Arcadia Publishing, 2004).

9. George Herbert Hildebrand, *Borax Pioneer: Francis Marion Smith* (Berkeley, CA: Howell-North Books, 1982).

10. Seymour Adler, *The Political Economy of Transit in the San Francisco Bay Area* (Berkeley, CA: Institute of Urban and Regional Development, 1980); Harry W. Demoro, *The Key Route: Transbay Commuting by Train and Ferry* (Glendale, CA: Interurban Press, 1985); Walter Rice and Emiliano Echeverria, *The Key System: San Francisco and the Eastshore Empire* (Charleston, SC: Arcadia Books, 2007).

11. *Hoover–Young Commission Report*, Part C, "Traffic Survey," July 19, 1930.

12. Raymond Forsyth and Joseph Hagwood, *One Hundred Years of Progress: A Photographic Essay on the Development of the California Transportation System* (Sacramento: California Transportation Foundation, 1998).

13. A succinct summary of highway financing is provided in C. V. Pavetti, "History of Highway Financing and Allocation Process in California," Highway Planning and Research Branch, California Department of Transportation, Sacramento, CA (1983).

14. Quoted in James L. Flink, *The Car Culture* (MIT Press, 1975), 141.

15. Forsyth and Hagwood, *One Hundred Years of Progress*, 20–21.

16. Col. John H. Skeggs, "The Modern El Camino Real," *California Highways and Public Works* (May 1930): 6–7.

17. Col. John H. Skeggs, "The Bayshore Highway Dedication," *California Highways and Public Works* (November 1929): 9–10, quote on p. 9.

18. Skeggs, "The Bayshore Highway Dedication," 9.

19. B. W. Booker, "Freeways in District IV," *California Highways and Public Works* (March–April, 1957): 1–18, quote on p. 1.

20. Col. John H. Skeggs, "Important Progress on East Bay Highways," *California Highways and Public Works* (July–August 1930): 14.

21. Booker, "Freeways in District IV," 1.

22. Skeggs, "Important Progress," 14.

23. R. E. Pierce, "American Canyon Cut-Off Opened; Will Save Hours between San Francisco and Capitol," *California Highways and Public Works* (November 1936): 28–29, quote on p. 28.

24. Even today, it requires excellent traffic conditions to facilitate a two-hour trip from Sacramento to San Francisco.

25. These hills are called different names in different locations. Where the Caldecott Tunnel was built, the range is generally called the Berkeley Hills.

26. The tunnel has been widened repeatedly since 1937, with a fourth bore that opened in 2014.

27. C. H. Purcell, "Californian Highway Expenditures as Compared with Other States," *California Highways and Public Works* (March–April 1929): 1–2.

28. Earl Lee Kelly, "Bridge Mighty Symbol of California Genius and Vision," *California Highway and Public Works* (November 1936): 12–13, quote on p. 13.

CHAPTER 2

How the Bay Bridge Was Planned in the 1920s

Although formal planning for the Bay Bridge did not begin until 1930, the idea of a bridge between Oakland and San Francisco received serious consideration throughout the 1920s. Indeed, the delays the project encountered throughout the 1920s can be seen as characteristic of megaprojects in general. In applying Frick's six C's test for megaproject status, the bridge envisioned in the 1920s passes. It was (1) colossal, dwarfing any bridge ever built in the United States up to that time; (2) costly, although the true cost was not realized at the time; (3) captivating, sparking the imagination of the region; (4) controversial, which was another reason it was not built during the 1920s; (5) complex; and laden with (6) control issues, which was the other reason the bridge was never built during those years. If nothing else, the frustrating failure of Bay Area leaders to build the bridge underscores how difficult megaprojects can be, and how remarkably successful the builders of the 1936 bridge were.

San Francisco as General Advocate for Transportation Improvements during the 1920s

The 1920s were a watershed in the development of all aspects of life in California. The economy of the state boomed with oil, agriculture, motion pictures, and other industries leading the way. The population of the state grew from 3.4 million to 5.7 million during that decade, although the majority of that growth occurred in Southern California. The population growth in San Francisco and Alameda Counties was nonetheless impressive, climbing from 850,000 in 1920 to 1,125,974 in 1930, an increase split roughly equally between the two counties.[1]

If the decade was a turning point in population growth and economic activity in the Bay Area, it was also an era in which optimistic visions of the future enthralled the civic and political leaders of the region. Author Daniel P. Gregory observes, "After World War I, San Francisco's outlook began to shift away from rebuilding and toward expansion. Faith in the future, in progress and growth, was strongly reinforced by evidence of how far the city had already come."[2]

The economic boom during the 1920s resulted in and, to a significant degree, was fueled by major increases in automobile ownership and use. The general increase in automobile use and economic growth went hand in hand.[3] The growing economy induced both population growth and increased automobile registration. The automobile in turn facilitated a pattern of industrial and population dispersal that was unthinkable in earlier decades. The confluence of these trends was most pronounced in Southern California, where population centers developed into what has been called a "fragmented metropolis."[4] In the Bay Area the trend toward population and workplace dispersal was less pronounced but nonetheless significant. While the automobile might have been less important in the development of the Bay Area during this decade than it was in Southern California, private vehicular use was emerging as the key growth element in the transportation network of the region.

In terms of planning in the Bay Area, the 1920s can be seen as a period in which civic leaders for the first time dared to dream of solutions to problems that had plagued the region for nearly a century. Great plans were made during this decade and a few were actually implemented. Most plans, however, were postponed until the 1930s or the years after World War II.

The problems faced by transportation planners were specific to the geography of the Bay Area—the series of bays and mountain ranges that separated the many communities in the region. The Bay Bridge was but one of a series of monumental transportation projects planned or built during this decade. As mentioned earlier, other massive transportation projects from the 1920s include the Carquinez Bridge, the Caldecott Tunnel, the Golden Gate Bridge, the Dumbarton Bridge, the San Mateo Bridge, expansion of the San Francisco Municipal Railway, great expansion of the Key System in the East Bay, construction of the Bayshore Highway on the Peninsula and the East Bay Highway in the East

Bay, and many others. These many transportation projects had one thing in common: they conquered the natural barriers of the Bay. Another aspect most of them shared was that they were inspired and instigated by officials in the city and county of San Francisco, which took on the role of regional planning leader during this decade.[5]

The drive for regional planning gained momentum during this period of economic and population growth. Regional planning involved coordination on a host of major initiatives, most of which involved public works investments—highway construction, water development, mass transit, and so forth. In all these areas San Francisco took the lead, although many other smaller Bay Area communities were wary of the domination that might come from a San Francisco–led program. Perhaps the best expression of the challenges and opportunities of regional planning was expressed in a 1925 document written by Harland Bartholomew.[6] The *Bartholomew Report* emphasized the pressing need for coordinated action on transportation and zoning, even while recognizing the difficulty of achieving such cooperation in a region comprising dozens of sometimes parochial interests.[7]

A key figure in Bay Area public works and planning during this period was Michael M. O'Shaughnessy, who served as city engineer for San Francisco from 1912 to 1934. O'Shaughnessy's role in the development of San Francisco in some respects parallels that of William Mulholland in Los Angeles. During the early decades of the twentieth century, Los Angeles and San Francisco, fierce competitors for domination as civic centers in the state, undertook some of the most daring public works projects in the history of American cities. The best known of these were two huge aqueduct systems: the Owens Valley Project of the city of Los Angeles and San Francisco's Hetch Hetchy System.

This great era of public works investment did not end, however, with water development. M. M. O'Shaughnessy played an especially important role in San Francisco in that he was city engineer in charge of a wide range of public works, unlike Mulholland, whose work was largely restricted to water resources. Even while Hetch Hetchy was under construction, O'Shaughnessy was deeply involved in a range of transportation proposals, including

M. M. O'Shaughnessy. Courtesy of San Francisco
History Center, San Francisco Public Library.

additions to the municipal railway system, construction of major
highway tunnels, and realignment of many city streets.

The most dramatic highway improvements pursued by San
Francisco during the 1920s were the structures to be called the
Bay Bridge and the Golden Gate Bridge. As Daniel Gregory notes,
the broad consensus in San Francisco for civic improvement
was most evident in public support for building these two great
bridges: "Support for civic beautification was combined with an
aggressive boosterism, to create an atmosphere of excitement and
urgency about the future. Commercial rivalries with Los Angeles
and other cities heated up. Bridges, in particular, became synony-
mous with future growth and prosperity."[8]

Leaders in San Francisco played two roles in the eventual construction of these great bridges: a generalized support for their
construction, whether by San Francisco or by another party; and
specific planning for their construction—again, whether by San
Francisco or another party. M. M. O'Shaughnessy was directly
involved in planning both bridges, although his role was quite

different in each case. He got involved with the Golden Gate Bridge almost by accident. In the mid-1910s he met J. B. Strauss, the chief engineer for the Golden Gate Bridge, when Strauss was in San Francisco to supervise construction of an amusement ride for the Panama–Pacific International Exposition, a ride based on the general engineering principles of a bascule bridge. Although remembered today chiefly for his work on the Golden Gate Bridge, Strauss in the early decades of the twentieth century was nationally known for his patented bascule bridge designs. O'Shaughnessy would commission two Strauss bascule bridges in the Mission Bay district, on 3rd and 4th Streets over Mission Creek, both of which are still in operation. At that time O'Shaughnessy discussed with Strauss the idea of a bridge connecting San Francisco with Marin County across the Golden Gate. The idea stuck with Strauss and he became a tireless promoter of the bridge until it was ultimately constructed two decades later. O'Shaughnessy, although a strong supporter of the bridge, did not participate actively in the long campaign to sell the bridge idea to wary taxpayers in Northern California counties.[9] O'Shaughnessy was much more directly involved in planning for the Bay Bridge, as detailed below.

The efforts of the city and county of San Francisco were not restricted to those of elected officials or appointees. Throughout the 1920s private business organizations provided key financial and political support for construction of both transbay structures. The initial exploration of the Bay floor for foundations of the Bay Bridge alignment, for example, was funded by the San Francisco Motor-Car Dealers, who mounted a spirited campaign for the Bay Bridge. The San Francisco Chamber of Commerce was resolute in its support for the Bay Bridge, particularly after Leland Cutler took over leadership of the group.[10]

The Specific Roles of Private and Civic Leaders from San Francisco in Planning the Bay Bridge during the 1920s

San Francisco's part in planning the Bay Bridge goes well beyond the general support and financial backing discussed earlier. Through an old California law, San Francisco reserved legal jurisdiction over a private toll bridge, an important fact during the

1920s, when it was presumed a private bridge offered the best
chance of being constructed. Under state law at the time, counties
were charged with approving private bridge franchises within
their jurisdiction. In the not-uncommon event that a toll bridge
crossed from one county to another, the franchise authority rested
with the jurisdiction on the left bank of the crossing, which in
the case of the San Francisco–Alameda County facility was San
Francisco.[11]

The fact that only private proposals were considered during
the 1920s was consistent with trends in major bridge construction throughout the United States during these years. Beyond the
Bay Bridge and the Golden Gate Bridge, three more major bridges
were planned or built in California during the 1920s: the Carquinez Bridge, the Dumbarton Bridge, and the San Mateo Bridge.
All were privately funded and operated. In the absence of other institutional arrangements, only private toll structures were deemed
feasible during this decade. By the end of the 1920s, however,
local and state transportation planners in California grew more
optimistic about the prospects of publicly built major bridges,
based on the success of the Benjamin Franklin Bridge (originally
named the Delaware River Bridge), which had been funded with
toll revenue–based bonds. During most of the decade, however,
planners at all levels of government proceeded under the assumption that only private bridges were feasible. That assumption governed the activities of private and civic leaders in San Francisco
who advocated in favor of a bridge to Oakland.

Various private proposals made their way to the city and
county of San Francisco in the years just before and after American involvement in World War I. Because they had jurisdiction
over a possible toll bridge franchise, San Francisco city officials
pursued the matter vigorously. In 1921, with thirteen different private toll bridge applications in hand, San Francisco officials applied to the War Department to initiate the process of obtaining
the necessary federal permits to span the navigable waters of San
Francisco Bay.[12]

Prior to making this formal application, the city contracted
with two notable private engineers to explore the floor of the
Bay. As noted, the funds for this contract came from the San

Francisco Motor-Car Dealers. The contract was given to John Vipond Davies and Ralph Modjeski. Davies was well known for having designed several of the early tunnels in New York City. Modjeski was known for his long and high bridges throughout the United States. Modjeski would later serve as chair of the Board of Consulting Engineers that led the design work for the Bay Bridge in the mid-1920s. The foundation work completed by Modjeski and Davies provided an early warning for all potential bridge designers that the Bay crossing was going to involve heroic engineering challenges.

In October 1921 the War Department conducted public hearings on the various private proposals. In December of that year that department issued general guidelines or rules that it would follow in assessing any permits for a bridge between the East Bay and the Peninsula. The War Department edict must have stunned both the private applicants and the officials from San Francisco. It laid out five conditions for any bridge under consideration, conditions that ruled out nearly every application then in play. The conditions were these:

1. No bridge of any kind will be approved north of Hunters Point.
2. No low bridge will be approved north of San Mateo.
3. A tunnel will be approved at any location if kept below a depth of fifty feet and if proper provisions are made for taking care of tidal prism.
4. A combined bridge and tunnel would be approved if the tunnel were kept below a depth of fifty feet and if a three-thousand-foot open channel is left on the San Francisco side, suitable provision being made for the tidal prism where bridge and tunnel join.
5. No more than one crossing is to be approved at present north of San Mateo.[13]

These criteria were problematic because they foreclosed consideration of more than half of the proposals made for a bridge alignment, including the one that was ultimately built. The War Department's conservative stance sought chiefly to defend commercial shipping lanes as well as free movement by military craft in serving the important bases scattered throughout the Bay Area. In retrospect, we can conclude the department's fears were unfounded; the Bay Bridge was built before American involvement in World War II and it greatly facilitated, rather than impeded, the movement of goods and military vessels during the frenetic wartime years.

San Francisco leaders responded by essentially ignoring the War Department edict. Throughout the 1920s the city entertained proposals for a transbay bridge, whether or not it conformed to the War Department guidelines. The situation was detailed in a long article in the *Engineering News–Record* in 1926. By that time the city had received seventeen proposals; that number would grow to thirty-eight by 1938. The seventeen proposals received by 1926 illustrate the broad attention this project had gained and the diversity of opinions about how the crossing could be made. The proposals included the services of some of the most famous civil engineers in the world at the time: Ralph Modjeski, John B. Leonard, J. B. Strauss, Charles Derleth Jr., W. L. Huber, C. E. Grunsky, George Goethals, J. A. L. Waddell, Gustav Lindenthal, and others.[14] Many engineers served on more than one team: Modjeski was on three and Goethals and Lindenthal were on two each. As a measure of the expertise these proposals attracted, the various engineering teams included the engineer of record for the Golden Gate Bridge (Strauss), the Benjamin Franklin Bridge (Modjeski), the Hell Gate Bridge (Lindenthal), and the Panama Canal (Goethals). The teams also included two of the five engineers (Modjeski and Derleth) who would form the Board of Consulting Engineers when the Bay Bridge was built by the state in the mid-1930s.

The bridge alignments for these proposals varied radically. The *Engineering News–Record* article discussed the alignments of fourteen of the seventeen proposals. Of these, four proposed an alignment that would later be called the southern crossing that lay between Hunters Point in southern San Francisco and various points in the city of Alameda.[15] Three alternatives went from the Key System Mole to Yerba Buena Island (the eastern span alignment selected in the 1930s) but touched down at various locations in San Francisco, north of Rincon Hill. The remaining alternatives left Alameda County from the Oakland Mole or the Alameda Mole and touched down at various spots in San Francisco between Rincon Hill and Pier 70.

The proposed alternatives also involved a wide array of bridge types. These were summarized briefly in the article in *Engineering News–Record* and were likely very conceptual in nature. Seven proposals called for "high steel trusses," presumably through trusses and not cantilevers, because cantilever bridges are called out separately from other trusses. There were three proposals for cantilever bridges, including an unusual plan by J. B. Strauss that featured a cantilever bridge linked with a bascule movable span. There were two proposals for suspension bridges and several plans that involved tunnels linked with high bridges.

At this point San Francisco leaders were feeling some of the anxiety that commonly accompanies what we now call mega-projects. The proposals were so numerous as to boggle the imagination. Despite rock-solid support from the business leaders in the Bay Area, the project was impossible to control. The War Department was resolute in opposing a bridge that linked the major population centers of Oakland and downtown San Francisco. San Francisco officials clearly intended to challenge that general guidance by submitting a specific bridge franchise plan for consideration. But San Francisco leaders were not equipped to select among the dozens of proposals, even those prepared by some of the most famous engineers alive. To overcome the War Department's reluctance, those leaders wanted to find the best possible bridge location and design to present. To establish some control over an increasingly uncontrollable situation, the city and county of San Francisco elected to spend $40,000 of city money (nearly $500,000 in 2013) to try to arrive at a preferred location and bridge type for the structure.

The team selected to conduct this study comprised Robert Ridgway, Arthur N. Talbot, and John Galloway; the team was known as the Ridgway Board. Galloway was a native-born Californian who, among other accomplishments, had served as chief engineer for the giant Healy–Tibbitts Construction Company. Talbot was a retired professor of civil engineering at the University of Illinois. Ridgway, the chair of the board, was chief engineer of the

Board of Transportation in New York City. The team was selected
for its expertise and in part because none of its members was associated with any of the bridge proposals then under consideration.

The trio released their findings in an extensive document,
dated May 5, 1927, commonly called the *Ridgway Report*.[16] The
report was informed by detailed traffic studies as well as engineering studies. The team addressed the three key issues that would
dominate all subsequent studies for the bridge: location, bridge
type, and traffic mix (specifically whether to include rail traffic).
It also struggled with two issues that would haunt all planning
for the bridge: the uncertain geology of the Bay floor and the
equally uncertain prospects for funding the bridge's colossal construction costs.

With respect to location, the Ridgway Board preferred an
alignment that differed from any proposed by private applicants
and from the alignment that was ultimately built. The board
looked at three points in San Francisco and three points in the
East Bay. In San Francisco, the points were Telegraph Hill, between Lombard and Bay Streets; Rincon Hill (where the 1930s
bridge is anchored); and a spot in what is now called Dogpatch,
near Pier 90. On the East Bay side, the board considered three
take-off points: the Key System Mole (where the existing East
Span touches down); the Alameda Mole; and a point at the foot
of Pacific Avenue, about midway on Alameda Island. The board
considered only straight east–west alignments: the Key System
Mole to Telegraph Hill, the Alameda Mole to Rincon Hill, and
Pacific Avenue to Dogpatch. These alternatives were assigned
numbers, based on the preferences of the board members. The
Alameda Mole to Rincon Hill route ranked highest (Alternative 1),
the Pacific Avenue to Dogpatch second (Alternative 2), and the
Key System Mole to Telegraph Hill last (Alternative 3). It will be
observed that the 1930s engineers eventually built on this finding but mixed the touchdown points for Alternatives 1 and 2 by
connecting the Key System Mole in the East Bay to Rincon Hill in
San Francisco. It appears that the Ridgway Board rated the alternatives strictly on level of service and not on the difficulties involved in building one alternative over the others.

With respect to the mix of traffic, the board considered variations on three traffic modes: main line rail service, interurban

rail, and cars and trucks. The board quickly dismissed the idea of taking main line rail traffic because of the high cost of building a bridge capable of carrying heavy rail loads and because the approaches on both sides of the Bay would need to be excessively long to accommodate rail grades. The board was adamant, however, that the bridge should carry both interurban and vehicular traffic. Indeed, much of the rationale for the board's preference for the Oakland Mole–Rincon Hill alignment was the ease of connections for interurban lines as well as the more difficult car and truck connections at the Dogpatch and Telegraph Hill touchdowns in San Francisco. Stated differently, the board preferred the Alameda Mole–Rincon Hill alignment because it was the best route for multimodal traffic. That multimodal commitment never wavered in the nine years between publication of the *Ridgway Report* and completion of the Bay Bridge.

As to bridge type, the board strongly favored a cantilever span on the west crossing and a bascule or some other type of movable span on the east. It concluded that a suspension bridge was infeasible owing to physical conditions of the crossing, chiefly its unstable foundation. It recommended instead long cantilever spans for the shipping channels near San Francisco and simple truss spans on the east, except for inclusion of a movable span to accommodate shipping in the East Bay.

The board summarized its preference for the Alameda Mole–Rincon Hill alignment as follows:

> It affords the most available direct route between the business centers; all the existing interurban lines may reach the bridge; the Alameda and Oakland termini reach the principal traffic highways; the San Francisco terminus is accessible from the entire street system of the city and is close to the business and shopping districts; interurban and main lines passenger stations may be provided; there is storage space for interurban cars; the land values on Rincon Hill are not high; no obstacles are placed across Oakland Harbor; there is no interference with the projected Alameda harbor; the largest existing wharves on the San Francisco water front lie seaward of the bridge; the clearances are all that commercial interests require;

there is no interference with the proposed Alameda Naval Base and only minor interference with the naval anchorage works; the existing ferry lanes are left free; Rincon Hill is an excellent point on which to terminate the bridge; any future rapid-transit system can easily be connected to the interurban system; and the present street-car systems can easily be diverted to the terminals.[17]

To a remarkable degree, the Ridgway Board presaged the discussions that would lead to the design of the 1936 bridge. They firmly established that interurban and vehicular traffic would be carried on the bridge but not heavy rail. They showed clearly that Rincon Hill was a favorable terminus in San Francisco because it connected with the commercial and shopping districts and because land was cheap in this low-income neighborhood. The board established that the East Bay Terminus should be near the Key System line, although they resisted connecting directly with the Key System Mole because it would require a forty-five-degree bend in the bridge; the designers of the 1936 bridge solved this by making that bend at Yerba Buena Island, allowing the bridge to locate at the much busier interurban terminus at the Key System Mole. The board also established that the cantilever bridge type would be useful for providing a shipping channel, although it envisioned the cantilever on the San Francisco side rather than the East Span. It was wrong about the unsuitability of a suspension span and recommended a movable bridge near Oakland, something that would have proven unworkable during the hectic years of World War II and the vast expansion of the Port of Oakland in the postwar era.

Despite its success in deciding important aspects of the bridge location, type, and traffic mix, the board failed completely to address two issues that would haunt bridge designers and planners in the 1930s and again at the end of the twentieth century. The first problem was how to build bridge foundations in the unstable floor of the Bay. The second was the vexing issue of how to pay for this colossal structure. By leaving these matters undecided, the Ridgway Board simply passed on to others the serious business of how to get this bridge built.

With regard to the Bay floor and finances, the board contended these two issues were inseparable because it was impossible to make any decisions about the cost of the bridge, or even the bridge type, without a much better understanding of what lay below the waters of the Bay. The board offered no speculation about what would be found on the Bay floor except to say that the Bay "must be expected to present great difficulties and extremely expensive construction" and that "at best the building of the piers will be a difficult and hazardous undertaking."[18]

The 1920s Experience of the City and County of San Francisco in Planning a Megaproject

Of the six C's spelled out by Karen Frick, it was control that ultimately spelled the doom of efforts by San Francisco officials to get a Bay Bridge built in the 1920s. The other C's were less problematic. Certainly the project was colossal; that was the very nature of the undertaking. It was understood to be costly but not such that it deterred private investors from lining up to build it. The project was captivating, capturing the attention of the largest investment firms and most famous engineers of the time. It was controversial only to a degree. The smaller communities in the Bay Area resented the aggressive role of San Francisco in this effort but at the same time likely appreciated that someone was taking the lead. The conflict between federal officials at the War Department and local officials in the Bay Area was also a nagging distraction. For the most part, however, controversy did not kill this project. The project was complex, to be certain, but not to an extent that San Francisco officials and dozens of private investors refused to take it on.

It was the issue of control that ultimately killed the project, at least for the time being. The Ridgway Board understood that there were a series of decisions that needed to be made and that these decisions needed to be made in a logical order. Nothing could proceed until the Bay floor was explored. Knowledge of the Bay floor would allow the bridge planners for the bridge to begin estimating the cost and selecting the bridge types. But it all came down to confusion about who was actually planning this bridge. San Francisco officials did as much as they could to organize the effort. But they could not select a bridge franchisee until they had information about the Bay floor. And they could hardly pay for the exploration of the Bay on their own, or ask any one of the applicants to fund this work. It was unlikely that the War Department would take control of the effort, since it essentially opposed any feasible alternatives.

It was a lack of control that killed this phase of megaproject planning, more than any other single factor. Then the stock market crashed a few months after the *Ridgway Report* was released. Any hope of a private bridge franchise collapsed with the Dow Jones average. What emerged as an alternative, however, was a vision of control of this huge project by the state and federal governments, including a specific arrangement called the Hoover–Young Commission that offered the degree of control needed to bring the project into the realm of feasibility. This unique federal–state partnership ultimately brought the situation under control and allowed the Bay Bridge to be built.

Notes

1. These population figures are taken from the *Hoover–Young Commission Report*, 74.

2. Daniel P. Gregory, "A Vivacious Landscape: Urban Visions between the Wars," in *Visionary San Francisco*, ed. Paolo Polledri (San Francisco, CA: San Francisco Museum of Modern Art, 1990), 78–103; quote on p. 78.

3. The close relationship between the growth of automobile use and economic prosperity in the 1920s is a central focus in James L. Frick, *The Car Culture* (Cambridge MA: MIT Press, 1975).

4. Robert M. Fogelson, *The Fragmented Metropolis, Los Angeles, 1850–1930* (Cambridge, MA: Harvard University Press, 1967). See also Scott Bortles, *Los Angeles and the Automobile: The Making of a Modern City* (Berkeley: University of California Press, 1987).

5. The leadership role of San Francisco is emphasized in Mel Scott, *The San Francisco Bay Area: A Metropolis in Perspective* (Berkeley: University of California Press, 1985).

6. Bartholomew, 1889–1989, was one of the key exponents of urban planning in the United States in the twentieth century. A civil engineer by training, his special focus was on transportation planning.

7. Scott, *The San Francisco Bay Area*, chap. 12; Harland Bartholomew, "The San Francisco Bay Region: A Statement Concerning the Nature and Importance of a Plan for Future Growth," San Francisco, CA, 1925.

8. Gregory, "A Vivacious Landscape," 86.

9. John Van der Zee, *The Gate: The True Story of the Design and Construction of the Golden Gate Bridge* (New York: Simon & Shuster, 1986); Kevin Starr, *Golden Gate: The Life and Times of America's Greatest Bridge* (New York: Bloomsbury Press, 2010).

10. The role of San Francisco business interests and Leland Cutler in particular in support of the Bay Bridge is discussed in detail in William Issel, "New Deal and Wartime Origins of San Francisco's Postwar Political Culture: The Case of Growth Politic and Policy," in *The Way We Really Were: The Golden State in the Second Great War*, ed. Roger W. Lotchin (Champaign, IL: University of Illinois Press, 2000), 68–92. Cutler would become a leading figure in various New Deal agencies during the 1930s. His advocacy for the Bay Bridge was recognized when the city and President Roosevelt asked him to moderate the ceremonies on the bridge's opening.

11. This obscure legal authority is discussed in an article written by the engineers in charge of the Bay Bridge for an engineering journal. C. H. Purcell, Charles E. Andrew, Glenn B. Woodruff, "San Francisco–Oakland Bay Bridge: A Review of the Preliminaries," *Engineering News–Record* (March 22, 1934), 371–77; quote on p. 371.

12. Ibid., 371.

13. Ibid.

14. "San Francisco Bay Bridge Projects Total 17," *Engineering News–Record* (October 28, 1926): 720.

15. At the time, these were the only likely alternatives under the strict War Department guidelines.

16. Robert Ridgway, Arthur N. Talbot, and John Galloway, "Report of the Board of Engineers, Transbay Bridge, San Francisco, May 1927." San Francisco 1927, hereafter the *Ridgway Report*.

17. Ibid., Scott, *The San Francisco Bay Area*, 211–12.

18. "Downtown Location Recommended for San Francisco Bay Bridge," *Engineering News–Record* (May 19, 1927), 821–22.

CHAPTER 3

How the Bay Bridge Was Finally Approved

The Hoover–Young Commission

Throughout the 1920s decision-making for the Bay Bridge was centered at the local level, with local governments (especially San Francisco's) taking the lead in prolonged but unsuccessful efforts to authorize a private bridge across the Bay. Those efforts collapsed with the onset of the Great Depression. The optimism that spurred interest in the bridge in the 1920s gave way to a gloom that had local and state governments happy just to survive.

The Depression also served to empower the federal government to take over many activities traditionally housed at the local and state levels, with one major objective in mind: putting people back to work. It is no accident that some of the greatest public works projects ever built in the United States were constructed during the 1930s, when spending on public improvements was seen as the best available countermeasure to combat massive unemployment. Although President Franklin Roosevelt is most closely associated with countercyclical spending, it was his predecessor, President Herbert Hoover, who initiated some of the grandest public works projects in California history, including the Bay Bridge and the Central Valley Project. If there is one person who brought order to the considerations of the Bay Bridge, it was Hoover. If there was one development that made the bridge-building process controllable, it was the appointment of the Hoover–Young Commission in 1929.

Hoover's Role as Champion of the Bay Bridge

The presidency of Herbert Hoover is the subject of considerable historical controversy. Until the 1970s historians generally concluded that Hoover did little to combat unemployment during the early and most difficult years of the Great Depression. Newer interpretations emphasize that Hoover simply had a different approach to combating unemployment, one built around long-lasting public works investments. These big projects, of which the Bay Bridge is an excellent example, produced worthwhile contributions to the communities in which they are located; at the same time, though, the projects were slow to ease unemployment because of the long lead times required to plan them.[1] Roosevelt adopted more fast-acting employment projects, such as those funded by his Works Progress Administration (renamed the Works Projects Administration in 1939), which were more effective in providing immediate short-term relief. The Bay Bridge was championed by Hoover as a great public works project and employment engine but was not completed until the end of President Franklin Roosevelt's first term.

Hoover's interest in the Bay Bridge actually predated his presidency. Hoover was both an engineer and a Californian, both of which no doubt contributed to his interest in the discussions of the Bay Bridge during the 1920s. Hoover was also an influential political leader long before he was elected president in 1928. Between 1921 and 1928 he served as secretary of commerce under Presidents Harding and Coolidge, during the years in which San Francisco sought to build the bridge. As commerce secretary Hoover threw his support behind the efforts of San Francisco, recognizing the importance of the proposed structure to the economy of the Bay Area. He believed he could help reconcile differences between Bay Area leaders and the War Department, one of the chief impediments to construction. Hoover recalled years later, "I attempted to conciliate the military and engineering conflicts, but my authority, without the backing of the President, was insufficient. Also, opinion in the Bay cities concerning the proper and feasible route was divided, and acrimonious debate was going on. At that time there seemed to be no way of financing a project so ambitious as this."[2]

This situation changed dramatically when Hoover ran for president in 1928. Campaigning in San Francisco, he openly endorsed the bridge and promised to work for its construction. Elected with broad support from California, Hoover acted quickly to fulfill that promise. There is reason to believe Hoover would

Herbert Hoover. Courtesy of Library of Congress.

have advocated for the bridge even had the country not slipped
into an economic emergency. The depression only increased the
argument in favor of building the Bay Bridge, even though Hoover
had taken major steps to support the project before the stock
market crash in late October 1929.

Within months of his March 1929 inauguration, Hoover had
begun discussions with California governor Clement C. Young
on two massive public works projects that had been debated in
California throughout the 1920s: the Bay Bridge and the Central
Valley Project. Ultimately, Hoover and Young called for creation of
two commissions—each called the Hoover–Young Commission—
to study how the state and federal government could cooperate
in completing the projects. Both commissions would ultimately
succeed but in widely divergent manners. The Bay Bridge was
completed as a state project in 1936; the Central Valley Project was
built as a federal undertaking, with most of the work completed
in the 1940s and 1950s.

Hoover announced the creation of the Hoover–Young San
Francisco Bay Bridge Commission in a press conference on August

13, 1929, several months in advance of the stock market crash and ensuing economic panic. In doing so, Hoover expressed support for the structure as a long-term stimulus to the economy of the Bay Area:

> There can be no question as to the necessity of such a bridge for the economic development of these communities. In addition to the cities of San Francisco, Oakland, and Alameda, the Governor of California through recent legislation has recently taken an interest in this problem. In order that we may have an exhaustive investigation with a view to a final determination which I hope will be acceptable to all parties, I have consulted with the Secretary of War and Secretary of the Navy as well as Mr. [Bert] Meek, the representative of Governor Young, and I shall appoint a Commission comprising two representatives from the Navy, two from the Army, and I shall ask the authorities of San Francisco to appoint one member, authorities of the east side of the Bay to appoint another member. I shall ask the Governor to appoint one of two members and I shall appoint a leading citizen, Mr. Mark Requa if he will undertake it, in the hope that we may arrive at a determination of the common interest.[3]

With that presidential pronouncement, the commission was established and the Bay Bridge given arguably its most important sign of political support.

Members of the Hoover–Young Commission

As Hoover promised in his announcement, the Hoover–Young Commission would comprise representatives from the Army and Navy, along with appointees from San Francisco, the East Bay, and the state of California. He also indicated at the outset that Mark Requa would chair the commission. Requa had three important qualifications for the job: he was an old friend of the president, he was a prominent California Republican, and he was an engineer with a lifetime of professional accomplishments. Hoover also appointed Charles D. Marx, an engineering professor at Stanford University who had taught Hoover as an undergraduate.

C. C. Young. Courtesy of Library of Congress.

Although he had retired in 1929, Marx was a respected member of the engineering community and close to the president. In the view of one historian, Marx's appointment "signaled the army and the navy that their representatives on the commission must be open-minded and not tied to traditional prejudices against a trans-bay bridge."[4]

The commission included two members each from the Army and the Navy: Rear Adm. Luther E. Gregory, U.S. Navy (Ret.); Rear Adm. W. H. Standley, U.S. Navy; Brig. Gen. G. B. Pillsbury, U.S. Army; and Lt. Col. E. L. Daley, U.S. Army. George T. Cameron, the editor of the *San Francisco Chronicle*, represented San Francisco, and state senator Arthur H. Breed represented Alameda County. The least-known but most active member of the commission was its secretary, Charles H. Purcell. Purcell was, in 1929, the highway engineer of the California Division of Highways, the equivalent of the director of Caltrans today. In terms of his administration of the design team, Purcell can be seen as one of the individuals most responsible for the design and construction of the Bay Bridge. Although he would head up the division of highways through the early 1950s, Purcell in 1929 was a relatively new arrival, having just been appointed as highway engineer the previous year.

It is difficult to overestimate the importance of the Hoover–Young Commission in getting the Bay Bridge built. The commission played a pivotal role in deciding the location of the bridge, the basic geometry of the bridge (particularly with respect to horizontal and vertical clearance), and its finances. In short, the commission both established the conceptual design of the bridge and decided how it would be paid for.

Recognizing the significance of what the commission accomplished, it is surprising how seldom the commission actually met and discussed these huge issues. It first convened on October 7, 1929 in the office of Governor Young. It continued to meet on October 8 and 9 before adjourning until July 22, 1930. It met three times in July of 1930 before issuing its final report on August 6, 1930. The commission disbanded once the report was released.

Role of the Bridge Department, California Division of Highways, in Commission Deliberations

In retrospect, it is clear that the commission met rarely because it had excellent staff work provided by the Bridge Department of the division of highways. The commission, which likely had limited funding to do its work, turned to the only state agency with experience in bridge design.

The first action taken by the Hoover–Young Commission was to request the division of highways, a unit within the Department of Public Works, to perform all necessary studies to support the commission's work. The initial motion read, "Resolved that the Department of Public Works of the State of California be asked to make an engineering, economic, and traffic study and furnish the Commission with all data obtained for the purpose of determining the relative value of the several proposed locations for a connection between San Francisco and Alameda counties."[5]

This resolution had the effect of making the Department of Public Works staff to the commission. Because the department had a small staff of its own—it was an administrative body in charge of various functional divisions—it turned to the division of highways, which had an extensive staff with experience in engineering, economic analysis, and traffic studies.

The timing of this request was excellent. Between 1929 and 1931 the state of California took a number of key steps to forward the cause of building the Bay Bridge; most of these events are discussed in detail in the following chapter. With respect to the Hoover–Young Commission, the key development was the creation of the California Toll Bridge Authority (CTBA) in 1929, just prior to the convening of the Hoover–Young Commission. The CTBA Act, in addition to creating an authority to build the bridge, appropriated $50,000 (nearly $700,000 in 2013 values) to study its feasibility. The CTBA consisted of five high-ranking elected or appointed officials, with little staff. It turned the appropriated money over to the division of highways to generate the studies requested by the Hoover–Young Commission. At that point, the division of highways was essentially staff to both the Hoover–Young Commission and the CTBA, giving it responsibility for all early planning for the Bay Bridge.

The division of highways in turn assigned most of the technical studies to its Bridge Division, a logical choice as that is where the bulk of its structural engineers were employed. These early studies gave the Bridge Department engineers hands-on experience in the process of designing a very large bridge, something that was new to most of them. Years later, the responsibility for the actual design of the bridge—taking the structure from concept to construction—was reassigned to a new entity, called the San Francisco–Oakland Bay Bridge Division of the Department of Public Works (also known as, and hereafter called, the Bay Bridge Division). Many of the engineers who worked on the early Hoover–Young studies would follow this work and transfer from the Bridge Department in Sacramento to the Bay Bridge Division in San Francisco.

Charles H. Purcell, the highway engineer (director of the division of highways) and Charles Andrew, bridge engineer for the division of highways, headed up the Hoover–Young studies, assisted by the staff of the Bridge Department and some private consultants. Their work took place in a period of about eight months. Given limited time and resources, Purcell and Andrews decided to build on the findings of the 1927 Ridgway Report, which they cited repeatedly in the 1930 final report of the commission. It will be recalled that the Ridgway Report emphasized the need to answer two key questions: What was the condition of the Bay floor? and, How will the bridge be financed? Purcell and Andrew spent most of their energies on providing answers to those two questions. They also reopened the question of the alignment of the bridge, depending on the analysis of the Bay floor and the financing issue, both of which affected the choice of an alignment. Purcell and Andrew also attempted to define the appropriate bridge types, although that issue remained largely unresolved when the commission released its final report in 1930.

Location Studies and Data from Borings

Regarding the uncertainties of the yet unexplored Bay floor, the 1930 *Hoover–Young Commission Report* observed, "The wide expanse of the bay across which any bridge must pass was unprospected as far as depths to suitable foundation were concerned. This fact was noted by Mssrs. Talbott, Ridgway and Galloway, in their 1927 report. No intelligent cost estimate could be arrived at until such borings were made, and even the possibility of building a bridge could not be determined on any complete line."[6]

The first order of business, then, was to conduct borings, a task that was contracted to the firm of Duncan–Harrelson, an active Bay Area construction company. Before the borings could be conducted, however, the Bridge Department needed to decide on a range of possible alignments. Again, Purcell and Andrew turned to the Ridgway Report to limit the range of options. The Ridgway Report had looked at three straight-line alternatives. The Bridge Department mixed and matched the termini of those three alignments, arriving at seven alternatives to guide the foundation studies. We next discuss each of these alternatives separately.

Locations No. 1-A, 1-B, and 1-C
from *Hoover–Young Commission Report*

- Location No. 1: The three Location No. 1 alternatives extended from Alameda to San Francisco, differing only as to the terminus in Alameda. In San Francisco, the proposed terminus was Rincon Hill, the location ultimately selected (Location 1-A). In Alameda, the terminus was the Alameda Mole (Location 1-B), and Location 1-C, which had a slightly different takeoff point in Oakland. All variations on this location traversed from Alameda to San Francisco;

C. H. Purcell. Courtesy of Library of Congress.

they differed only on how traffic would be brought from the
mainland in Oakland to Alameda Island. Location 1 was the
preferred alternative in the Ridgway Report.

- Location No. 2: This alternative, also found in the Ridgway
  Report, connected Alameda to a spot in what is now called
  Dogpatch in San Francisco, about halfway between Rincon
  Hill and Hunters Point.
- Location No. 3: The third Ridgway Report location termi-
  nated at the Key System Mole on the East Bay side and at
  Telegraph Hill in San Francisco.
- Location No. 4: The Bridge Department devised Location
  No. 4 by mixing the termini in Locations 1 and 3, selecting as
  the East Bay terminus the Key System Mole and, as the San
  Francisco terminus, Rincon Hill, with Yerba Buena Island
  providing a midpoint termini for two separate bridges. This
  was the alternative ultimately selected and built.
- Location No. 5: This location terminated at Hunters Point,
  near the southern edge of San Francisco, and at the southern end of Alameda Island. Although rejected in 1930, this
  location would be restudied in the 1950s and dubbed the
  southern crossing.

The mixed results of the Duncan–Harrelson borings delivered both encouraging and discouraging news for every alignment. Bedrock was absent on parts of every proposed alignment, ensuring that at least some part of any bridge would be founded on sand. In the end, Location 4 was selected as the least discouraging of seven generally bad alternatives.

The studies began by eliminating Locations 1, 2, and 5 on the basis of depth to bedrock. To satisfy the War Department and the obvious requirements of maritime trade, the state would need to have at least one shipping channel crossed by very long spans, which could only be supported on piers founded on bedrock. At Locations 1, 2, and 5, bedrock was reached only on the west side of the crossing (near San Francisco), and then only at depths "beyond the reach of practicable foundations."[7]

The borings on the west side of Yerba Buena Island were much more encouraging along Locations 3 and 4. At key pier sitings, depth for Location 3 (leading to Telegraph Hill) was −211 feet—that is, 211 feet below the water level. At Location 4 (leading to Rincon Hill), the depth was only −163.5 feet. The engineers concluded that the path from Yerba Buena Island to Rincon Hill traversed a "high ridge of shale and sandstone," a fortuitous development because the Yerba Buena to Rincon Hill route also enjoyed economic and traffic service advantages.[8] The discovery of this ridge of bedrock ensured that the Bay Bridge would be built between Rincon Hill and the island.

East of Yerba Buena Island, the news was uniformly bad on every alternate location. The borings typically extended down more than three hundred feet and rarely made conclusive contact with bedrock. This was true of Locations 3 and 4 (Locations 3 and 4 were coterminous between Yerba Buena Island and Oakland). Three borings were made east of Yerba Buena Island, with bedrock encountered at very great depths except near the island, where more-favorable depths were found. Reading these data, the report's authors concluded that it was likely that a long-span structure could be founded on bedrock just east of the island but nowhere else. As discussed later, the *Hoover–Young Commission Report* used these borings to make suggestions as to bridge types. The 1930 report described in nearly exact detail the bridge that eventually would be constructed between Yerba Buena Island at the east shore, which the authors believed was the only bridge type that could be supported on the foundations of the East Span. "East of Goat [Yerba Buena] Island the cantilever spans adjacent to the island can be founded on shale. The remaining part of the structure is composed of 300-foot viaduct spans and can be safely supported on piles driven into sandy clay."[9]

The foundation studies, for all practical purposes, determined where the bridge would be built and what it would look like. On the East Span in particular, the borings dictated that a single long span would be built next to the island, linked to a series of small viaduct spans. Meanwhile, the discovery of the shale ledge on the West Span helped planners to conclude that a suspension bridge—the preferred bridge type for very long crossings in the 1930s—could be supported and likely would be built. The foundation borings, in short, allowed engineers to select general bridge types, which, in turn, enabled them to make dependable cost estimates and look ahead to potential financial vehicles.

Traffic Studies and Their Impact on Bridge Location and Bridge Type

The second critical concern of the Hoover–Young Commission was an assessment of traffic patterns, to ensure the Bay Bridge would provide the greatest good to the greatest number of potential customers. The traffic studies, as discussed earlier, were conducted by Lester Ready. Ready's analysis was fundamentally a study of commuters to San Francisco. He spent very little time analyzing traffic from San Francisco to the East Bay. From the outset, bridge planners understood that the chief traffic demand was for a quick round-trip commute between suburban homes in the East Bay and businesses in San Francisco, a demand that was great enough to warrant constructing the bridge and collecting the tolls needed to pay for the bridge.

The Ready report indicated clearly that the densest concentration of San Francisco commuters lived in the metropolitan area comprised of Berkeley, Oakland, and Alameda, where people commuted to San Francisco both by automobile and interurban rail. Predictably, the interurban commuters were clustered in neighborhoods that were well served by the trains, whereas automobile commuters lived in more distant neighborhoods that were not easily accessed by train. The term *distant* meant something far different in 1930 than it does today. For example, Ready classified everyone living south of Oakland in a single zone for his analysis and that zone accounted for 6.6 percent of automobile commuters and less than 2 percent of interurban commuters.

The principal conclusion from the Ready report was that the bridge should terminate near the focal point for each end of the commute. For the East Bay, that focal point lay somewhere in Oakland, easily accessible from Alameda and Berkeley. The other focal point was downtown San Francisco, which centered on Montgomery Street but radiated for a considerable distance in all directions. This conclusion supported both Locations 3 and 4, both of which began in Oakland and ended either on Telegraph Hill (Location 3) or Rincon Hill (Location 4). Location 4 proved to be preferable, at least in part because real estate was much cheaper at Rincon Hill.

Ready's analysis predicted significant changes in regional transportation resulting from a bridge, but greatly underestimated the degree to which construction of the span would alter Bay Area commuting and other traffic patterns. The analysis foresaw two major changes over time: the collapse of the ferry system, especially the automobile ferries; and diversion of commuters from the interurbans to automobile commuting. The collapse of the ferry system was predicted based on experiences elsewhere. The Benjamin Franklin Bridge connecting Pennsylvania and New Jersey was completed in 1922. Its construction resulted not only in a total collapse of the river ferry system, but also in an explosion of automobile traffic that far exceeded the number of autos that had been carried on the ferries.[10]

As to diversion of traffic away from the interurban rail network, this impact was expected because of the differential in travel time, automobile commute versus interurban commute. The automobile user could expect a savings of thirty minutes in each direction thanks to the bridge, versus without the bridge, whereas interurban commuters gained fewer than ten minutes. "Increased vehicular traffic and deflection of passengers from interurban trains may be expected," Ready observed. As noted earlier, he projected that vehicular crossings of the bridge would increase to 12.6 million each year by 1950, and that interurban traffic would diminish correspondingly.[11] The actual results, however, were far more dramatic. By 1950 the transbay traffic had increased to 33 million crossings, nearly three times what Ready had predicted, and the diversion from the interurbans was so great that the Key System teetered on the verge of collapse. The last Key System trains crossed the bridge in 1958.[12]

Studies of Bridge Types and Other Structural Issues by the Hoover–Young Commission

As a final matter, the division of highways engineers working for the Hoover–Young Commission had to grapple with the design for the bridge, at least to determine whether a bridge could be built for the $72 million budget. The section of the report dealing with design was one of the smallest, although it likely required the greatest commitment of time. Section 3, "Design Data," comprised a mere nine pages in a report that totaled 209 pages. In that brief and concise text, however, the state engineers confronted the major issues that would haunt their successors from the 1930s through the early 2000s: "The essential design criteria considered by staff to the Commission were: capacity (number of lanes for vehicles and trains); horizontal clearance (distance between piers); vertical clearance (height between deck and water level); and grades. By the time this section was written, the division of highways engineers had decided on Location 4 as the preferred alternative, so the discussion of design criteria that follows is largely restricted to how they applied to that alternative."[13]

In terms of vertical clearance, the engineers assumed the need for a mid-channel height of 220 feet, which could accommodate any commercial or military ships that might enter the Bay. As for the grades, the recommended inclines were 3 percent for railroads and 3.5 percent for vehicles.

In considering horizontal clearance, the division argued for a shipping channel span of at least 1,600 feet on the San Francisco side and 650 feet on the Oakland side. This disparity reflected the fact that the Port of San Francisco was still the principal commercial harbor in the Bay Area. It did not, however, consider the fact that Oakland's harbor was quickly gaining business and overtaking San Francisco, nor did it take into account the War Department's desire to protect military shipping on the East Bay side. The recommendation for 1,600 feet on the west side and 650 feet on the east made its way into the final Hoover–Young Commission finding but not into the eventual design. As built in the mid-1930s, the Bay Bridge featured equal 1,600 feet shipping channels below both crossings.

As to the bridge's carrying capacity, the report recommended "a capacity of six lanes for highway traffic and at least two operative and one passing or emergency track for interurban trains."[14] To achieve these requirements, the division of highways engineers offered two alternative arrangements for vehicular and train lanes. One would have featured six lanes of general vehicular traffic (cars and trucks) on the upper deck and four lanes of railroad track on the lower. The other (the one actually built) involved six lanes of automobile traffic on the upper deck with two railroad tracks and two truck lanes on the lower deck. Both alternatives included sidewalks on the upper deck.

The report also devoted several pages to describing the complicated approaches, or distribution systems, on both the East Bay and San Francisco sides. Being highway engineers first and foremost, the authors of the report respected the awesome task involved in getting traffic on and off the structure, particularly if truck, automobile, and train traffic required separate portals at each terminus.

As a final matter, the division of highways engineers attempted to project the bridge types that would best fit the design criteria. Here, no doubt, Purcell and Andrews understood that it was premature and speculative to decide on bridge types because neither had any experience designing very large bridges and because they lacked much of the technical data required for a bridge type decision. Nevertheless, they offered recommendations that seemed to fit the bill: four 1,700-foot through cantilevers on the west crossing and one 720-foot deck cantilever joined with twenty-one steel deck spans on the east side. These recommendations would have resulted in a bridge completely unlike the one actually built, and, one suspects, neither Andrews nor Purcell was upset that their sketchy suggestions were not followed.

On balance, the Hoover–Young Commission was remarkably successful in settling the thorniest issues facing the bridge project: where the foundations were best able to support the bridge, the best location from a structural as well as a functional standpoint, and the upper limit of bonded indebtedness the bridge would support. The only area where the studies were ignored had to do with bridge type. As discussed later, a powerful and learned Board of Consulting Engineers, with dozens of years of experience in designing some of the largest and most famous bridges in the world, accepted the commission's finding with regard to the foundation and location of the bridge, but ignored altogether its recommendations as to bridge type.

The Hoover–Young Commission as a Model for Planning Megaprojects

The Bay Bridge of the 1930s was assuredly a megaproject, more so even than the East Bay span of the 2000s, which involved less than half the work associated with the original Bay Bridge. The 1930s bridge was built, however, on time and within budget and with little controversy. Much of the ease with which the bridge was built can be attributed to the fact that the Hoover–Young Commission comprised representatives of most of the parties that could have contributed to potential controversy or who might have made demands that would have put the project behind schedule or over budget. President Hoover and Governor Young figuratively locked the important players in a room and did not let them out until they agreed on how the bridge should be built and paid for.

Going back to Karen Frick's six C's for megaprojects, the 1930s bridge was certainly colossal, was very costly, was captivating to all involved, and was inherently complex, from the foundations to the approach spans. What it was not, however, was controversial or bedeviled with control issues. Controversy was always just below the surface: the friction between the War Department and state officials, the jealousies of East Bay cities and San Francisco, potential tensions between automobile commuters and train commuters and truck drivers, and any number of other potential flashpoints.

The Hoover–Young Commission avoided these potential pitfalls in three ways. First, it was clear from the outset that the commission spoke for the president and the governor, an alliance only rarely accomplished before or since. Local interests and private parties could only buck that formidable alliance at their own risk. Second, the specific composition of the commission helped ensure that many of the potential controversies were resolved before the commission's report went public. The greatest example here was the resolution of the friction between the War Department and local interests, since both were amply represented on the commission and the final report would necessarily reflect consensus on major issues. Similarly, the nonmilitary representatives carried enough diversity to steer away from strictly local controversies. The four local representatives—Mark Requa, Charles Marx, George Cameron, and Arthur Breed—were capable of speaking for their respective interests but were also widely respected as statesmen, capable of defending the common good. Finally, the commission deferred to the division of highways for counsel on all technical matters. There was no room for dueling engineering opinions, as happened so frequently with the replacement of the East Span in the early twenty-first century. Charles Purcell and Charles Andrew earned the respect of the commission by providing thorough and altogether trustworthy advice. Purcell and Andrew were admired in the 1930s to a degree never achieved by Caltrans officials in the 1990s and 2000s.

The Hoover–Young Commission achieved a unique blend of inclusiveness and exclusivity. Commission members spoke for the public and each was answerable to the unique public he represented (all members happened to be men). But each was also very much his own man and willing to speak for the broader good as well as the specific constituency he represented. It was a model more reminiscent of the Roman republic, where learned and wise representatives spoke for their constituencies, than of the modern American ideal of governmental transparency, where decisions are made only after exhaustive public hearings and lengthy environmental reviews.

The Hoover–Young Commission cut through the cords of controversy that had stalled the bridge for more than a decade and delivered sound advice to the two most important decision-makers: the president of the United States and the governor of California. While it did not eliminate all barriers, the commission did pave the way for final approval of the project over the next several years.

Notes

1. The Hoover historiography is discussed in James Stuart Olson, *Herbert Hoover and the Reconstruction Finance Corporation, 1931–1933* (Ames: Iowa State University Press, 1977).

2. Quoted in Robert Hessen, *Herbert Hoover and the Bay Bridge: A Commemorative Essay* (Stanford, CA: Hoover Institute, 1986), 4.

3. Quoted in ibid., 5.

4. Ibid.

5. *Hoover–Young Commission Report*, 5.

6. Ibid., 99.

7. Ibid., 118. For Location 1, the depth was −229, i.e., 229 feet below mean high tide. At Location 2, the depth was −293. At Location 5 it was −235.

8. Gregory, "A Vivacious Landscape," 78.

9. *Hoover–Young Commission Report*, 125.

10. Ibid., 54.

11. Ibid., 53.

12. Ready's traffic predictions formed the basis for financing the bridge. The economic analysis of the bridge, a separate section within the larger *Hoover–Young Commission Report*, used Ready's forecasts as a way of predicting income from the bridge. Using Ready's forecast of 12.6 million crossing in 1950 and a toll of 65 cents, the economic analysis concluded that the toll income could support a construction cost of $72 million. That figure formed the basis for Reconstruction Finance Corporation bonds and generally served as the upper limit budget for the bridge. *Hoover–Young Commission Report*, Sec. 4 (Economic Studies).

13. *Hoover–Young Commission Report*, Sec. 3, "Design Data."

14. Ibid., 160.

CHAPTER 4

The Context of Great Bridges—Part 1

From the 1920s and 1930s

The Bay Bridge was designed and built near the end of what was one of the most remarkable eras in American bridge construction, the decade from the mid-1920s through the mid-1930s, when some of the most important and best-known bridges in the United States were erected. Periodically, the pace and scale of bridge construction has accelerated, as bridge engineers, public financiers, and highway planners learn from and build on prior accomplishments. During these periods of quickened activity, the pent-up demand has been satisfied by constructing bridges across the most difficult crossings. The 1870s and 1880s represented one such period of prodigious bridge construction, including the Eads Bridge in St. Louis and the Brooklyn Bridge in New York. The decade from about 1927 to about 1937 certainly qualifies as an era of extraordinary bridge-building activity.

This decade was notable for the extent to which individual bridge engineers were granted authorship of their spans, much like the notable architects who became nationally famous during the same period. This individual recognition is surprising given the fact that very large bridges require a great deal of collaborative design, with the need for collaboration increasing proportionally to the size of the bridge. During this extraordinary decade (1927–37) there emerged a small group of engineers who achieved popular recognition and individual attribution for their efforts.[1] Leon Moisseiff, Ralph Modjeski, David B. Steinman, O. H. Ammann, J. B. Strauss: while not household names, these engineers were widely recognized and praised for their work. Rarely before or since have bridge engineers been treated to such celebrity status.

Eads Bridge, St. Louis. Courtesy of Historic American Engineering Record Collection, Library of Congress.

This era might also be seen as the birth of the revenue bond and public authority, an innovative combination that emerged as the funding strategy of choice for the construction of great bridges. The building of very large bridges has always been constrained by the capacity of private developers or governmental agencies to pay for them. Nearly all of the great bridges from the 1920s and 1930s were financed through revenue bonds, usually issued by a stand-alone public authority, in which the construction bonds were guaranteed by the revenue from bridge tolls. This seemingly prosaic development in public finance contributed as much as any technological advance to the accelerated rate of construction during this period.

Finally, the decade can also be seen as the era of the suspension bridge and, to a lesser degree, the cantilever bridge as the bridge types of choice for very long spans. The decade began with construction of the Carquinez Bridge in 1927, which helped

Benjamin Franklin Bridge. Courtesy of Carol M. Highsmith, Library of Congress.

revive interest in cantilever bridges following decades of disasters involving that type. The bulk of the great bridges during this period, however, were suspension bridges—the Benjamin Franklin Bridge (1926), built just prior to this decade, the Golden Gate Bridge (1937), and, of course, the West Span of the Bay Bridge (1936). The Bay Bridge is especially notable because it incorporated both of the dominant bridge types of this era.

All great bridges from this 1927–37 period contributed in some way to the success of the Bay Bridge. These spans were also important to the Bay Bridge in that many of the engineers who designed them also served on advisory boards for the Bay Bridge.

The Carquinez Bridge is an unusual example of the important bridges from this period because it was privately financed and because it is a cantilever. Built by the American Toll Bridge Company, this bridge was initially conceived in 1922 and was open to traffic by 1927. This hurried pace was possible in part because the bridge was privately funded and in part because it was a less complicated span than many from this era. The simplicity of the bridge is only apparent, however, in relation to the other great bridges of this era; the Carquinez crossing is very wide and high with a busy shipping channel beneath that requires a main span of at least 1,100 feet. The engineers for the project were Charles Derleth Jr. and David B. Steinman. In most general histories, Steinman is credited with the cantilever design for this bridge, a type he selected only after he was convinced a suspension bridge was inappropriate for the strait.[2] Although Steinman had no role in designing the Bay Bridge, Derleth was a member of the consulting board. Steinman and Glenn Woodruff, the engineer of design for the Bay Bridge, would collaborate later on the great Mackinac Bridge in Michigan.

The Benjamin Franklin Bridge between Philadelphia and Camden, New Jersey, was built at about the same time as the Carquinez Bridge. Construction was delayed, however, through numerous preliminary designs, with various cantilever and suspension spans contemplated. When construction began in 1921, however, it was of a suspension bridge that was designed by a team featuring Ralph Modjeski as the chief engineer and Leon Moisseiff as the engineer of design. The Benjamin Franklin was

George Washington Bridge, Manhattan. Courtesy of Historic American Engineering Record Collection, Library of Congress.

also a landmark in bridge finance: it required a bi-state commission (later an authority) to handle its bonds sales and construction. It was also a great achievement in suspension bridge design: its 1,750-foot main span was the longest at the time it was built, although that distance would be eclipsed quickly by other great bridges from this decade.[3]

The George Washington Bridge across the Hudson River between Manhattan and New Jersey was the last great American bridge to be built before work commenced on the Bay Bridge and Golden Gate Bridge. As such, it was the bridge most often cited as a model by the designers of the Bay Bridge. The George Washington, like the Benjamin Franklin, stood as something of a milestone in public financing, having been built by the Port Authority of New York and New Jersey, a bi-state authority with broad powers for public works construction. It was also a milestone in the history of suspension bridge design; the great main span was twice that of the Benjamin Franklin Bridge.

The design of the George Washington Bridge is generally attributed to O. H. Ammann, the chief engineer for bridges for the Port Authority. Ammann assembled a distinguished team of consulting engineers, including Daniel Moran, Leon Moisseiff, and J. B. Strauss. Moran was selected for his experience in dealing with difficult foundations, while Moran was generally considered the dean of bridge foundation work. Moisseiff, in addition to his earlier work on the Benjamin Franklin Bridge, had gained considerable attention for his ability to calculate stresses in very long suspension spans. Both Moran and Moisseiff would play similar crucial roles in crafting the Bay Bridge, with Moran essentially designing the foundation work and Moisseiff performing all final checks of stresses, particularly on the suspension spans.[4]

The Golden Gate Bridge is the bridge to which the Bay Bridge is most often compared because the two are in close proximity and were under construction at the same time. Like the Bay Bridge, the Golden Gate Bridge became famous for its engineering superlatives, including the fact that it had by far the longest suspension span in the world. The bridge has also been widely praised for the gracefulness of its design and its spectacular scenic location. The two bridges had been planned and debated for about the same length of time, from early planning in 1921 through construction in 1936–37. The Golden Gate Bridge was in some respects even more difficult to finance than were the other bridges in this group. It was ultimately funded by creation of a unique special district that comprised a group of California counties from San Francisco northward. The design of the Golden Gate Bridge went through several radical shifts, beginning with an early Strauss idea for a combined cantilever-suspension span that one writer called an "eyesore."[5] The graceful design that was ultimately built evolved over the 1920s as Strauss worked with engineer Charles Ellis and others.

When it appeared that financing was finally in place, Strauss assembled a distinguished group of consulting engineers, many of whom had worked on other great bridges during the decade and who would soon work on the Bay Bridge. Strauss' consulting

Huey P. Long Bridge, New Orleans. Courtesy of Historic American Engineering Record Collection, Library of Congress.

engineers on the Golden Gate included O. H. Ammann of the George Washington Bridge; Leon Moisseiff, who had worked on many great bridges; and Charles Derleth, who had worked on the Carquinez Bridge and others.

There were numerous other bridges built during this decade that had some bearing on the design of the Bay Bridge. The Kill van Kull (or Bayonne) Bridge between Staten Island, New York, and Bayonne, New Jersey, was also built by the Port Authority under the direction of O. H. Ammann. He was assisted by a board that included Daniel Moran, Leon Moisseiff, and J. B. Strauss.[6] Ralph Modjeski also designed the Huey P. Long Bridge in New Orleans, which was under construction the same time as the Bay Bridge, while Daniel Moran worked on the span's tricky foundations in the bed of the Mississippi River.[7]

The historical significance of the Bay Bridge is not diminished when assessed within the context of the dozens of great American bridges constructed during this decade. It is a fruitless exercise to attempt to establish whether any one of these great bridges is ultimately more important than the others.[8] The Bay Bridge was regarded as a great challenge by everyone involved with it, particularly the engineers of the state of California, none of whom had previously worked on a span of this magnitude. It is a testament to their good sense that they brought to the design team a distinguished Board of Consulting Engineers. The members of that team had worked together on many of the other great bridges of this era, and brought their individual and collective skills to bear on what was the most expensive of any of the bridges of this era, and in some ways the most complex and daunting.

Notes

1. The historiography of great bridges is extensive. One of the most entertaining and reliable of such works is Henry Petroski, *Engineers of Dreams: Great Bridge Builders and the Spanning of America* (New York: Vintage 1995).

2. This history of the Carquinez Bridge is told in great detail in David B. Steinman and Sara Ruth Watson, *Bridges and Their Builders* (New York: Dover Publications, 1941).

3. Ralph Weingardt, *Engineering Legends: Great American Civil Engineers* (Reston, VA: ASCE Publications, 2005).

4. These engineers are featured in Petroski, *Engineers of Dreams*, and Weingardt, *Engineering Legends*. The plain steel towers of this bridge were intended to be clad in stone but were left bare for the sake of economy.

5. Van der Zee, *The Gate*, 48.

6. This great steel arch structure is scheduled for major renovation because its vertical clearance is insufficient for modern large tankers and cargo ships.

7. This bridge was recently widened to essentially double its original width.

8. The Bay Bridge does stand above the others in the collective judgment of the engineers of the American Society of Civil Engineers (ASCE). In 1955 the ASCE selected the "Seven Wonders" of American engineering, its official list (at that time) of the most important engineering landmarks. The Bay Bridge is the only bridge on that list.

CHAPTER 5

How the Bay Bridge Was Designed

1931 to 1933

There is a curious habit among bridge historians to attribute bridge design, even the design of massive structures like the Bay Bridge, to individuals, in the way in which building designs are attributed to individuals such as Frank Lloyd Wright, Frank Gehry, and so forth. Henry Petroski makes this case in a qualified manner in *Engineers of Dreams:* "Though it is true that no individual engineer, no matter how great, can single-handedly do everything—from detailed calculation to supervision of construction—required to bring a major span to fruition, great bridges do appear to have had masterminds behind them, albeit masterminds with many helper minds."[1]

This drive to assign primary if not sole authorship probably confuses as much as it illuminates. Even the Golden Gate Bridge, so truly masterminded by Joseph Strauss, was hardly his work exclusively, even at the mastermind level. To conclude otherwise is to overlook the great contributions of Leon Moisseiff, Charles Ellis, Irving Morrow, and others. The folly of seeking individual authorship is illustrated graphically by the attempt to assigning credit for the Bay Bridge. Shortly after the bridge was built, the popular press gave exclusive credit to Charles H. Purcell, the chief engineer. A glaring example was a series of paeans, published in book form in 1937, called *Purcell Pontifex: A Tribute.*[2] More recently, bridge historians have tended to assign responsibility elsewhere a bit more widely. Donald Jackson, in *Great American Bridges and Dams*, gives credit to Purcell and Glenn Woodruff, the engineer of design and third-ranking member of the Bay Bridge Division.[3] In his history of California in the 1930s, *Endangered Dreams*, Kevin Starr gives greatest credit to Woodruff, assisted by other "straightforward civil servants" working for the state.[4] Henry Petroski does not attempt to assign authorship but rather laments the fact that one person led the effort: "Among the reasons for its relative obscurity must also be counted the fact that this bridge had no single prominent and dominant dreamer like a Roebling, Lindenthal, Ammann, or Strauss serving as executive director and providing a visible personality to the project."[5]

This chapter will address how the Bay Bridge was designed. At the most basic level, it will attempt to set the record straight as to who was involved in designing the bridge and to correct the terrible neglect of the dominant role played by Ralph Modjeski. At a more abstract level, the chapter will analyze the design criteria used by engineers in laying out this structure and how these criteria were used to solve the most vexing problems of the Bay Bridge: the extraordinary length of the bridge in total and the individual lengths to Yerba Buena Island; and the daunting task of building foundations that were deeper than anything previously attempted.

The first and most crucial aspect of this bridge's design is that it occurred in a great hurry. Although some planning was accomplished during the 1920s and by the Hoover–Young Commission, the real design of the bridge, from type selection to construction drawings, took place in a twenty-four-month period, between early 1931 and early 1933. The project was intended, at least in the minds of many political leaders, as a way to put unemployed men back to work. While it was useful to hire young engineers to do design work, the point of the project from a jobs creation standpoint was to hire young laborers, carpenters, steel workers, and others by the thousands. With that overall objective in mind, the designers of this bridge were under enormous pressure to move the project from design to actual construction, and toward this end they performed with admirable success.

Establishment of the Bay Bridge Division in San Francisco

On state organizational charts, the Bay Bridge Division was a unique entity and something of an orphan. It was not directly associated with the division of highways, which operated and built all other state bridges. It was technically a part of the CTBA, which was essentially a shell organization of appointed and elected officials. The Bay Bridge Division was a stand-alone organization with one purpose: to design and then to build the Bay Bridge.

The CTBA was created by the California legislature in 1929 to plan, build, and operate the Bay Bridge. The word *authority* in its name reflected a fashionable trend in public works construction in the early 1930s in which relatively autonomous governmental agencies would borrow the funds necessary to build a large undertaking—a megaproject, in modern usage—and then repay those loans through tolls and other income streams. The Port Authority of New York and New Jersey was the most ambitious American authority, but others were established throughout the United States.[6]

The decision for an authority created an awkward relationship between the Bay Bridge Division and the division of highways, the forerunner of modern Caltrans. Since the early twentieth century, the design, construction, and maintenance of state highway bridges was the responsibility of the division of highways. By creating the CTBA in 1929 and then funding it with $650,000 in 1931, the legislature created a new state bridge design agency that rivalled or perhaps exceeded the scope of the bridge section of the division of highways.

As noted in an earlier chapter, the CTBA asked the division of highways to serve as staff for the Hoover–Young Commission. Thus, Charles Purcell, the director of the division of highways, and Charles Andrew, head of the bridge section, coordinated the Hoover–Young studies. In 1934 the CTBA and Earl Lee Kelly, the director of Public Works, created the Bay Bridge Division, charging it with spending what remained of the $650,000 to develop the bridge design.[7]

The new division, however, was hardly divorced from the division of highways. Kelly appointed C. H. Purcell to be chief engineer for the Bay Bridge, without asking him to relinquish his larger role as state highway engineer, the equivalent of director for the department. Thus, between the creation of the Bay Bridge Division in 1931 and completion of the bridge in 1936, Purcell wore both hats with the two closely aligned agencies.

Purcell was a bridge engineer by training and inclination, although he spent most of his career as an executive. Born in North

Bend, Nebraska, on July 27, 1883, Purcell studied engineering at Stanford University for a year but returned to Nebraska when his father died. There, he resumed his studies and graduated from the University of Nebraska in 1906.[8] Like many other young engineers at the turn of the twentieth century, Purcell moved to the West to pursue work in mining and with the railroads. He was chiefly interested in bridge engineering and in 1912 took a job with the newly created Oregon State Highway Department. His tenure there did not overlap with Conde McCullough, who designed many well-known Oregon structures. Purcell left the highway department in 1917 to take a job with the federal Bureau of Public Roads; McCullough came to the highway department the following year. In 1928 Purcell was appointed highway engineer for the California Division of Highways, a position he would retain until shortly before his death in 1951. In a quarter century as director, Purcell led the division of highways from its earliest years to the dawn of the freeway era.

Purcell in 1931 further solidified the link between the division of highways by hiring Charles Andrew as bridge engineer, essentially Purcell's chief assistant. Andrew was a full-time bridge engineer all of his adult life. He received his engineering degree from the University of Illinois in 1906. He moved to the West after graduation and rarely returned to the Midwest. Between 1906 and 1908 he worked on the great railroad bridge across the Willamette River at St. Johns, Oregon, serving under Ralph Modjeski, who was already developing a reputation as one of America's better bridge engineers.

Following his work with Modjeski, Andrew began a long career as a civil servant. His first public sector job was with the city of St. Johns. He later took a job with the U.S. Bureau of Public Roads, where he worked under C. H. Purcell. Between 1920 and 1927 he was a bridge engineer with the Washington State Highway Department. Then, in 1927, he was hired to head the Bridge Department of the California Division of Highways, where he was quickly reunited with Purcell.[9]

For a brief time, Purcell and Andrew were the only full-time employees of the new Bay Bridge Division. They quickly set out, however, to assemble a crew of engineers and other design

Charles Andrew, C. H. Purcell, and Glenn Woodruff, San Francisco–
Oakland Bay Bridge, 1936. Courtesy of San Francisco History Center, San
Francisco Public Library.

professionals. Initially, Andrew and Purcell were able to bypass
the usual civil service process, arguing that flexibility was needed
because specialized bridge engineers demanded more pay than
the state system allowed. In addition, they pointed out that
the work would last only a few years, and "past experience has
shown that it would be a heavy burden to give the necessary ex-
aminations."[10]

When the civil service waiver was granted, they immediately
hired Glenn Woodruff, who was then working in the office of
Ralph Modjeski in New York City. A native of Pennsylvania born
in 1890, Woodruff graduated from Cornell University in 1910. He
worked for the American Bridge Company, the Northern Pacific
Railroad, and the Lehigh Valley Railroad. After service in World
War I, he took a job with the prestigious consulting firm of Robinson and Steinman. Between 1923 and 1931 he was a principal engineer with Modjeski and worked on several signature Modjeski
structures, including the Benjamin Franklin and Huey P. Long

Bridges. He stayed with the Bay Bridge Division through completion of the project, and he continued to be active in bridge design until shortly before his death in 1974.[11]

Within a few months of setting up the Bay Bridge Division, Purcell, Andrew, and Woodruff had assembled a team of more than fifty workers, mostly engineers but also surveyors, draftsmen, and clerical staff. They continued to hire outside the civil service system until March 1932, when the state ruled that all civil service rules applied to the division, forcing them to make any new hires from civil service lists. The result was that the Bay Bridge Division took many new hires from the experienced ranks of civil service engineers at the division of highways.

This crew worked in a nice office building at 500 Sansome Street in San Francisco and stayed together during the design phase from 1931 to 1933. Many also stayed on as resident engineers and in other capacities during the construction phase from 1933 to 1936. In time, many would return to jobs in Sacramento with the division of highways.

The Board of Consulting Engineers

Purcell left behind no explicit explanation of why he and Andrew believed they needed a Board of Consulting Engineers, although the reasons are apparent, given the situation facing the Bay Bridge Division. First, it was customary within the engineering profession to rely on a distinguished panel of experts to approve the design of very large or complex bridges. Virtually every major bridge designed between 1927 and 1937 was governed by such a panel, with many experts serving on more than one board.

An equally persuasive argument is that no one at 500 Sansome Street other than Glenn Woodruff had any real experience in designing or building a very large bridge. Purcell and Andrew had designed dozens of bridges, some of them quite complicated, but they had no experience with the structure types likely to be used on the Bay Bridge. This no doubt was why they hired Woodruff, and this is also why they appointed and relied heavily on a Board of Consulting Engineers.

Purcell and Andrew began discussing the Bay Bridge with Ralph Modjeski before December 1930, and before most of the crew was in place on Sansome Street. Public Works director Earl Lee Kelly announced in December that he intended to appoint a board and that two members would include Ralph Modjeski, who would serve as chair, and Daniel Moran, a very experienced foundation expert from New York City.

Because there were problems with contracts, none of the Board of Consulting Engineers was actually working for the state until August 1931. It appears that Modjeski and Moran in particular were serving on a pro bono basis for much of 1931. In February 1931, for example, Purcell wrote to Modjeski asking his opinion on four alternative alignments between San Francisco and Yerba Buena Island. Modjeski replied shortly thereafter, offering refinements for the four alternatives that would help "from the standpoint of economy as well as aesthetics."[12] This early correspondence suggests that the two worked well together from the outset and that Purcell admired and respected the opinion of the elderly bridge master.

Modjeski is one of the best-known bridge engineers to have practiced in the United States during the first half of the twentieth century. His bridges are known for their beauty as much as their utility. As was observed in a 1931 tribute to him, "Ralph Modjeski was inherently an artist. He has not chosen oil, or dry point, or marble, or even music, in which he doubtless would have excelled, to express himself, but steel, stone, and concrete. Using these as his chosen media, 'by a pleasing simplicity of form and reliance upon the quiet dignity of the long spans whose members gracefully express function free from superfluities,' he has made of bridge engineers a recognized art without in the least minimizing its importance as a science."[13]

He was born Rudolphe Modrzejewski in Poland in 1861. His mother, Helena, was known as Madame Modjeska and was regarded as one of the great actresses of her time. Young Ralph traveled widely with his mother, including on her many visits to the United States. He settled with her in what is now called Modjeska Canyon in Orange County, California, living there between 1876 and 1878. In 1878 he moved to Paris, France, where he studied bridge engineering at l'École des Ponts et Chaussées. After graduation he returned to the United States, where he lived until his death in California in 1940.[14]

Ralph Modjeski. Courtesy of Historic American Engineering Record Collection, Library of Congress.

For several decades Modjeski specialized in railroad bridges. His major rail spans included a bridge across the Mississippi River and one across the Missouri River, both in 1905. He built several large railroad bridges in the Pacific Northwest, including one across the Willamette at St. Johns, Oregon, where he met Charles Andrew. His greatest success came with his plans for the Benjamin Franklin Bridge in 1926, and the Huey P. Long Bridge, which was under construction the same time as the Bay Bridge.

Purcell approached Daniel Moran at about the same time that he contacted Modjeski. Daniel E. Moran and his partner, Carlton Proctor, were arguably the best-known foundations engineers in the United States in the mid-1930s. Moran was born in New Jersey in 1864 and graduated from Columbia University in 1884. Like many other engineers of his generation, he began his career in railroad work, laying out the Nevada-California-Oregon narrow-gauge line between Reno and the most remote corners of California and Oregon. In the early 1890s, he turned to the specialized field of foundation work, where he would excel until he died, about a year after the Bay Bridge was completed. Before his work on the Bay Bridge, he had designed the foundations for most of the major bridges built in the decade, including the George Washington, Benjamin Franklin, Huey P. Long, and Triborough Bridges.[15]

Purcell had decided to hire Modjeski and Moran by late 1930 but was still undecided about a year later as to whom else to include. He wrote to Modjeski in July 1931, assuring him that "all major appointments in the designing organization will be made in consultation with you and that efficiency and ability will be the basis upon which an appointment will be made." In the same letter, Purcell floated two names for assistance in doing the calculations for the suspension spans: Holton Robinson and Leon Moisseiff.[16] Several weeks later Modjeski replied, suggesting that Moisseiff would be a better fit for several reasons: Modjeski was accustomed to working with him, and he was already working on the Golden Gate Bridge and was likely to be in San Francisco anyway.[17] As a measure of the confidence Purcell had in Modjeski, he hired Moisseiff a week after he got this letter.

Leon Moisseiff was born in Latvia in 1872. He began studying engineering in Latvia but immigrated to the United States before his studies were completed. He finished his degree at Columbia University in 1895 and began a very long career as a bridge engineer. In addition to his work on the Bay Bridge, he is credited with substantial contributions to the George Washington Bridge, Golden Gate Bridge, Mackinac Bridge, and the ill-fated Tacoma Narrows Bridge.[18]

The remainder of the Board of Consulting Engineers was filled by what Purcell called "local men." These were Charles Derleth, dean of the school of engineering at the University of California; and Henry Brunnier, a consulting engineer from San Francisco. In actual practice Purcell relied heavily on Modjeski, Moran, and Moisseiff, whom he called the "New York members of the Board," and largely ignored the advice of the two "local men."

Purcell turned to the New York members for specific tasks. If there was a question about foundations, he relied on Moran. For questions about suspension spans, he called on Moisseiff. Modjeski's role resembled what Petroski called the prominent dreamer or mastermind. Purcell turned to Modjeski to envision how the entire structure was going to work.

The communication between Purcell and the three New York members documents a complicated interplay between Purcell, who was obliged at all times to consider the budget and schedule, and the three master engineers, who could advise him on how to get the job done, given his financial and time constraints. Who designed the bridge? These four men, with Modjeski providing the inspiration and Purcell the perspiration.

Solving the Problem of the Bridge Type for the West Bay Crossing

Arguably the most vexing design issue was how to span the two-mile distance between San Francisco and Yerba Buena Island. The design challenge was both natural and regulatory. The natural problems were twofold: the sheer distance from one point to the next, and the incredible depth to bedrock for the foundations, which promised to eat up a huge part of the tight budget. The regulatory issue was the need to maintain War Department–dictated horizontal and vertical clearances. All of these factors argued for making the span with the fewest number of piers.

The challenge of the West Bay crossing caused Purcell to select the three New York members of the board. Modjeski was experienced in long suspension spans, as was Moisseiff. Moran was the master of deep foundations. Together, these three men guided Purcell in solving this most difficult part of the bridge design.

Although they briefly contemplated cantilever spans, the entire crew—the Bay Bridge Division on Sansome Street and the board members in New York—seriously considered only suspension bridge types for the West Bay crossing. The great length of the crossing, however, ruled out conventional suspension methods, even those used for very long crossings such as the George Washington Bridge.

By late 1931 the Bay Bridge Division and the New York members had settled on three basic options for conquering this massive span. One envisioned a conventional suspension bridge, with two anchorages on land and two at-sea piers. A second projected a continuous suspension bridge with more than two at-sea piers but fixed to the two land anchorages. And the third, the one finally built, involved a massive center pier that acted like a land anchorage, linking two suspension bridges. None of these had ever been built before. Although hundreds of conventional suspension bridges had been built, none came close to the spans required for a two-mile-long crossing. The individual spans were so great that engineers worried about their performance in winds and earthquakes, both of which haunted any bridge in this setting.

The team looked at two variations: one with three towers and one with four towers in the bay. In either case, the cables would have been strung for two miles, a fact that gravely concerned the engineers and resulted in the early rejection of this option.

Meanwhile, the ultimately selected double suspension span design looked promising from the outset but suffered from the fact that such a bridge had never been built or tested. The basic concept called for the building of five piers, with the centermost being a massive hunk of concrete so thick and heavy that it could act like a land pier, providing an anchorage for each side of the double suspension bridge.

Because the continuous suspension design was rejected early on, the essential choice facing the Bay Bridge Division and the consulting engineers lay between the extraordinarily long conventional suspension bridge and the double suspension design. In a manner that would presage discussions of the new East Bay span in the twenty-first century, the choice between the conventional suspension and the double suspension was framed as one pitting aesthetics against economics. Purcell and Modjeski favored the double suspension bridge because it functioned well, was aesthetically pleasing, and cost a great deal less than the conventional bridge: $2 million ($31 million in 2014 values).

Moran and Moisseiff were convinced that an extraordinarily long suspension span would be what planners in the twenty-first century would call a signature span. The two groups—Modjeski and Purcell on one side and Moran and Moisseiff on the other— would argue throughout 1931 over which way to go. In November 1931 Moran made one last plea to the board to adopt the spectacular spans of the long conventional bridge:

> We would further call the attention to the board to the greatest advantages, to the cities of San Francisco and Oakland, of a single span design; first, because it would provide

the best possible waterway for shipping and; second, because it would undoubtedly create a bridge which architecturally and spectacularly would appeal to the civic pride of both Cities, and would attract and interest all of the surrounding districts. In my opinion, such a bridge would attract so many visitors to the two Cities that in the course of years the profit to the two Cities, from this source alone, would more than compensate for the relatively small difference in cost. It would be impossible to estimate how much the City of New York and Brooklyn profited by the spectacular achievement of the Brooklyn Bridge, or how much St. Louis benefited by the Eads Bridge.[19]

That letter was sent in November 1931. In January 1932 the full Board of Consulting Engineers met and unanimously approved the double suspension bridge design. We do not know what exactly caused Moran and Moisseiff to change their minds, despite their obvious enthusiasm for the more "spectacularly" impressive idea of a very long suspension bridge. What is important, and what is so different from the experience with the 2013 bridge, is that the experts came together when it was necessary to do so, and supported a design that in their collective judgment made the most sense. And is there a bridge enthusiast alive today who can honestly say that the West Bay crossing, with its dramatic center pier and five-pier procession is not a beautiful structure? Moran and Moisseiff saw a chance for something truly special but risky to build. The board as a whole decided on something that was somewhat less spectacular but also less dangerous. The West Bay crossing was so designed.

Solving the Problem of the West Bay and East Bay Crossing Foundations

From the time of the Hoover–Young studies, all involved understood that the foundation work for this bridge was problematic. For the West Bay crossing the depth to bedrock was daunting but not insuperable to a foundations genius like Moran. The West Bay crossing was simply a challenge that someone like Moran likely welcomed.

The East Bay crossing, however, proved a much different matter. All indications were that bedrock was an inestimable depth below the Bay floor, so deep that borings could not reach it. The inability to reach bedrock governed every other decision having to do with the East Bay crossing.

By late 1931, when most of the decisions had been made about the West Bay crossing, Purcell, Andrew, Woodruff, and the others on Sansome Street were still at a loss as to what to do on the East Bay crossing. In November of that year, Purcell wrote to Moran, expressing his doubt that the East Bay piers could ever be taken to bedrock. Later that month Moran replied with a guarded conclusion that building the bridge on clay might be good enough: "We would agree that these piers could be safely designed to rest on very solid clay."[20]

In May 1932 the New York members of the Board of Consulting Engineers—Modjeski, Moran, and Moisseiff—met on several occasions to develop specific designs for the East Bay piers. They were particularly concerned about the three in-water piers that would support the cantilever bridge over the shipping channel; these were identified as Piers E-3 through E-5 (Piers E-1 and E-2 were on land). The group, with Moran no doubt taking the lead, selected very deep concrete caissons for these three critical piers, similar in design to the West Bay piers but not taken to bedrock. Although founded on stiff sands, the three caissons were nearly as deep as those on the West Bay crossing; Pier E-3 in particular was designed to go to –230 feet below sea level, while the deepest pier on the west was –240 feet.[21]

This memo illustrates two points that help differentiate the 1936 bridge from the 2013 bridge. First, in dealing with a subject so fraught with safety concerns, the Bay Bridge Division engineers deferred to the experts in New York. There was no thought of debating the design in public as in the case of the 2013 bridge; the decision was given to their experts and the expert opinion was honored. Second, although neither the 1946 nor the 2013 bridge was carried to bedrock, the main span of the 1936 bridge was founded on a massive concrete caisson, pushed hundreds of feet into the Bay floor. The 2013 bridge foundations for the signature span (at the location of the 1936 cantilever), is founded on piles.

The use of piles instead of a caisson was one major source of concern about the safety of the new bridge.[22]

Solving the Problem of the East Bay Crossing Superstructure

There is a persistent myth about the 1936 bridge, one that was cited repeatedly in public debate over the 2013 bridge. The myth held that San Francisco, as the economically and politically stronger city, was given graceful suspension spans to ponder, while working-class Oakland was given a workhorse cantilever bridge to observe. The myth is completely false with respect to the possibility of building suspension spans on the East Bay crossing. The cautious Board of Consulting Engineers never considered founding a suspension bridge on anything less than bedrock.

There was, however, a lively discussion among consulting engineers about whether the shipping channel span on the East Bay crossing should be a cantilever or some other, more aesthetically pleasing, form. This debate played out in private, just as did the debate over a continuous or double-suspension bridge on the West Bay. The engineers stated their differing opinions, took into account cost, safety, and buildability issues, and decided on the cantilever/truss design that existed until very recently.

In early 1931 Charles Andrew presented a speech to a group that is not named in the historical record but likely was an engineering organization. Andrew's address bore the technical title "Preliminary Foundation Studies and Main Span Design, San Francisco Bay Bridge."[23] With regard to the shipping channel of the East Bay, Andrew states, "Present superstructure plans east of the island contemplate a 1400 feet cantilever just off shore." In January 1932, however, Glenn Woodruff gave a speech that made it clear the decision as to bridge type had not yet been made: "Our principal design problem is, then, to find the most economical solution to the 1400 foot span and at the same time give due consideration to the question of appearance. We have considered three possibilities as follows: 1. A self-anchored suspension. 2. Cantilever. 3. Continuous. Our studies have not reached a point as to enable us to give a definite conclusion."[24]

As to these three types, the cantilever is easiest to visualize because it existed at the Bay Bridge until very recently. By "continuous," Woodruff meant a continuous deck truss system, essentially a long viaduct. The self-anchored suspension (SAS) span is intriguing because that was what Caltrans actually built in 2013, a design that has caused innumerable problems. As discussed in a later chapter, however, the early 1930s understanding of what an SAS bridge would look like was far different from the single tower that exists on the bridge today. It is quite likely that Woodruff had in mind a design similar to the Three Sisters in Pittsburgh, Pennsylvania, that were completed a few years before the Bay Bridge and that were widely regarded as good-looking bridges. In appearance, the Pittsburgh bridges strongly resembled conventional suspension bridges, although their anchorage systems were highly experimental at the time.

Between January and April 1932 the Bay Bridge Division and the Board of Consulting Engineers methodically analyzed various options for this span, even going beyond the three alternatives mentioned by Woodruff. On January 25, 1932, the Bay Bridge Division submitted a report, probably written by Woodruff, expressing dissatisfaction with the cantilever design and mentioning a new alternative: a tied arch. "None of the cantilever designs were satisfactory from the standpoint of appearance. The tied arch design was developed as presenting a better appearance. The estimates indicate that it compares favorably in cost with the cantilever design."[25] The board agreed and urged the division to pursue the tied arch, "if not materially more expensive."[26]

A tied arch is a common bridge type but not one commonly used for spans greater than one thousand feet. It is quite likely that the division and board had in mind something like the Hell Gate Bridge in New York City, completed in 1916 on plans by Gustav Lindenthal. Although a working railroad bridge, the tied arch structure was commonly seen as a handsome structure and it is likely the Hell Gate that the designers had in mind.

In April 1932 the Bay Bridge Division again presented a report to the Board of Consulting Engineers: "We have made several layouts in an effort to develop a structure more pleasing in appearance than a conventional cantilever. Among our early studies we developed a design for a self-anchored suspension bridge. The appearance of the resulting structure was not satisfactory and its cost was excessive. Our next effort was the tied arch design."[27]

Hell Gate Bridge, New York City. Courtesy of Historic American
Engineering Record Collection, Library of Congress

The report masks any internal disagreement within the Bay
Bridge Division but it is clear from this and other memos that
Woodruff, an experienced designer of big bridges, favored the tied
arch over the cantilever. It is also likely that he was overruled by
Purcell who, although a bridge engineer by training, was primarily
charged with bringing this massive project in on time and within
budget. The April 1932 report concludes, "It should be noted that
the same unit prices have been used in both the arch and cantilever design. It is our opinion that not less than $240,000 should be
added for more expensive fabrication and more difficult erection
of the arch span. This gives a differential of $600,000 in favor of
the cantilever design. We recommend that one of the cantilever
layouts be chosen for the final design and that further study of the
arch be discontinued."[28]

The $600,000 figure in 1932 equates to about $10.5 million in
2014 values. In the planning for the 2013 bridge, $10.5 million was

treated as if it were an inconsequential sum; the real differences got attention only when measured in billions of dollars. Bridge designers could argue for years over whether the tied arch was a better design, as Woodruff clearly believed, and whether it would have been worth $10.5 million for that better design. All we can conclude with certainty is that the difference in appearance was not worth $10.5 million to those who designed the bridge. And we can further conclude that it was a series of such decisions that helped bring the bridge in on time and slightly under budget, a rare and admirable occurrence among megaprojects of the twentieth and twenty-first centuries.

Notes

1. Petroski, *Engineers of Dreams*, 19.

2. Anonymous, *Purcell Pontifex: A Tribute*. No author is given for this work. This book, available at the California State Library, is noted as "Privately Printed by His Friends."

3. Donald C. Jackson, *Great American Bridges and Dams* (Washinton DC: Preservation Press, 1988).

4. Starr, *Endangered Dreams*, 328.

5. Petroski, *Engineers of Dreams*, 336.

6. A recent study explores the popularity of four such authorities: Peter Handee Brown, *America's Waterfront Revival: Port Authorities and Urban Redevelopment* (Philadelphia, PA: University of Pennsylvania, 2009).

7. As noted above, the Bay Bridge Division is the abbreviated name for the San Francisco–Oakland Bay Bridge Division of the Department of Public Works.

8. Anonymous, *Purcell Pontifex*, 1937.

9. Charles E. Andrew, "Professional Record," 000.051, California State Archives, Sacramento, CA.

10. Andrew to G. T. McCoy, 000.51, California State Archives.

11. "Glenn Barton Woodruff, F. ASCE," *Transactions, ASCE*, 139 (1974), 5880.

12. Ralph Modjeski to C. H. Purcell, February 17, 1931, Board of Consulting Engineers 200.5, California State Archives.

13. Quoted in Petroski, *Engineers of Dreams*, 172–3.

14. There is an extensive literature about both Ralph Modjeski and his mother. The bibliography in Petroski (*Engineers of Dreams*) lists most of the major works.

15. Memoir, "Daniel E. Moran," *Transactions ASCE* (1938): 1840–44.

16. Purcell to Modjeski, July 25, 1931, Board of Consulting Engineers, 200.5, California State Archives.

17. Modjeski to Purcell, August 15, 1931, Board of Consulting Engineers, 200.5, California State Archives.

18. Petroski, *Engineers of Dreams*, 293–5.

19. Moran and Proctor to Woodruff, November 9, 1931, Board of Consulting Engineers, 200.5, California State Archives.

20. Ibid.

21. "Memorandum," Moran and Proctor, Board of Consulting Engineers, 200.5, California State Archives.

22. This issue is discussed in detail in chapter 10 of this book.

23. "Preliminary Foundation Studies and Main Span Design, San Francisco Bay Bridge," Board of Consulting Engineers. California State Archives. Even the date of the speech is not recorded but its provenance suggests early 1931.

24. Glenn Woodruff, "The Design of the San Francisco–Oakland Bay Bridge," 000.0552, California State Archives.

25. "East Bay Crossing," January 25, 1932, Papers of Charles Derleth, Water Resource Archives, University of California, Riverside.

26. Minutes of the Board of Consulting Engineers, Sixth Meeting of the Second Session, January 27, 1932, in the papers of Charles Derleth, Water Resources Center Archives, U. C. Riverside.

27. *The East Bay Crossing*, March 18, 1932, report submitted to the Third Session of Consulting Board, April 18–22, 1932, 3–4. This report was dated March 1932, but was presented to the board in April.

28. Ibid.

CHAPTER 6

How the Bay Bridge Was Built

The 1930s

If there is one characteristic that distinguishes the 1936 from the 2013 Bay Bridge, it is the legendary, almost mythic quality surrounding the history of the construction of the New Deal bridge. The 2013 span has interesting construction stories, but they mostly have to do with unpleasant misfeasance by some state personnel and shoddy work by the Chinese contractors who fabricated much of the "signature span" of the structure. These are not the stuff of legend. The 1936 construction story is about stone-broke young American men, often dressed in suits and ties but more commonly in overalls, climbing onto steel platforms thousands of feet above the Bay, risking and sometimes losing their lives. There are no photographs of the building of the 2013 bridge that can match even one image of young men with no tethers, looking down on the Bay.

The other storied aspect of the 1936 bridge construction is that it was accomplished in three years and came in just a little ahead of time and slightly under budget. This indicates that, in addition to brave young men on steel girders, there were careful sharp-pencil guys at the state watching the budget, good project managers at the construction companies, dedicated quality control state employees—most of whom were on the same steel girders as the workers—and plenty of other control people who saw this massive job to a successful conclusion. If the 2013 bridge falls flat in comparison to the 1936 structure, it is most clearly in the area of control. The 1936 people controlled cost and quality; the 2013 people did not. The 1936 people did their job well; the 2013 people did not.

This is the story of how the 1936 bridge got built.

High steel construction. Courtesy of San Francisco History Center, San Francisco Public Library.

The Contractors

Not surprisingly, this project, valued in billions of dollars in 2014 values, attracted the attention of all major American construction companies, which had been mostly idle during the Great Depression except for those involved in big federally funded jobs, like the Hoover Dam. The state awarded seven contracts, numbers 2 through 8, in 1933.[1] The contractors for the seven major elements comprised three big groups. The first group comprised the steel makers, who won the contracts for the steel superstructure on the West Bay (Contract 6) and the East Bay (Contract 7). These accounted for nearly half the cost of the bridge. The second group included the concrete workers, who built the huge concrete jobs below the steel superstructure, including the substructure for the West Bay (Contract 2) and the East Bay (Contract 5). The concrete firms were associated with the Six Companies group (see below), and most had worked together on other huge federal jobs, including the Hoover Dam. The third group consisted of local contractors who won the jobs for building the San Francisco and Oakland approaches as well as boring the huge Yerba Buena Island Tunnel (Contracts 3, 4, and 8).

The steel contractors were led by the American Bridge Company, which had been organized in 1901 by the U.S. Steel Company. U.S. Steel also controlled a major subcontractor, Columbia Steel Company, which had an office in San Francisco. The prime value of the job was fabrication of the steel, which American Bridge did in its plants in Indiana and Pennsylvania. American Bridge subcontracted the fabrication of the East Bay superstructure to a competitor, McClintic-Marshall, a big subsidiary of Bethlehem Steel, that had built major parts of the George Washington Bridge and would later be a major fabricator for the Golden Gate Bridge.

The Six Companies group that did the concrete work for most of the bridge comprised an informal but powerful alliance of some of the most powerful construction companies on the West Coast: General Construction Company in Seattle, Morrison-Knudsen in Boise, Henry Kaiser in Oakland, McDonald and Kahn in San Francisco, Pacific Bridge Company in Portland, and J. F. Shea, also in Portland.[2]

The local contractors included Clinton Construction Company, which built the Yerba Buena tunnel and the Oakland approaches, and Healy–Tibbitts, which built the San Francisco approaches. Both had been in business in the Bay Area for decades before the contracts were let in 1933.

Building the West Bay Substructure

The deepwater piers of the West Bay crossing arguably posed the most complex and dangerous contract in that it involved the highest degree of unproven technologies. Contract 2 covered all the piers from San Francisco to Yerba Buena Island. The piers were numbered W-2 through W-6, with the W signifying west of Yerba Buena Island. W-1 was a land pier in San Francisco and was covered by a separate contract.

Although the Six Companies group won the bid, they relied on a large group of Bay Area subcontractors to get the job done. Moore Dry Dock Company, an Oakland firm that historically had built and repaired ships, was responsible for building the caissons for the foundation work. Judson Pacific and Western Pipe and Steel would actually fabricate the caissons. The workforce for this

West Bay caisson. Courtesy of San Francisco History Center, San Francisco
Public Library.

contract peaked at just under 1,000 men in 1934 and always exceeded 800 during the whole job.[3]

Pier W-2 was a conventional bridge pier and received no special mention among engineers. Piers W-3 to W-6, however, were
so difficult and structurally complicated that they earned great acclaim in the engineering journals of the time, chiefly because they
involved foundations taken to depths never before attempted or
achieved. The best of these articles appeared in *Civil Engineering*
and were written by Carlton Proctor, business partner to Daniel
Moran, who designed the pier work.[4]

The complex construction process that Moran invented and
attempted to patent was described by Proctor as a "domed coffer
dam with pneumatic false bottom." It was built around a metal
rectangle that surrounded a series of cylinders, each of which was
fifteen feet in diameter and fitted with a dome. The number of cylinders varied, depending on the size of the pier.

Each caisson was built on land in San Francisco and towed to
the job site and tethered with cables. A hemispheric dome was

welded atop each cylinder and each cylinder was pumped with forced air, causing the structure to float. Concrete was then poured into the voids outside the cylinders, causing the caisson to sink but at a rate controlled by the counteracting forced air. New sidewalls and cylinder lengths were added as the caisson sank. This process was repeated until the caisson hit bottom, or "landed."

Once the caisson was stabilized on the Bay floor, the domes were removed and the cylinders were repurposed as "dredging wells," or access points for clamshell buckets.[5] The process of dredging, pouring new concrete, building higher sidewalls and cylinders continued until the caisson was firmly on bedrock.

There was one great mishap involving these caissons. Pier 6 is just west of Yerba Buena Island and rests in the deepest water of all the piers. In mid-December 1933, the caisson "landed" and the contractors immediately began to dredge toward bedrock. On January 14, 1934, however, the caisson, which was more than 150 feet tall at this point, began to tilt, threatening to topple and be rendered useless. Daniel Moran quickly came from New York to San Francisco to supervise the emergency work. The clamshell buckets were used to cut down the western side of the floor to bring it in line with the lower eastern half. Divers were sent down to help direct the work. Tragically, one of the divers, Lloyd Evans, died at Pier 6 from the bends, or what bridge builders call "caisson disease."

Building the East Bay Substructure

The strategy for the East Bay caissons was quite similar to that on the West Bay, with three exceptions. The caissons were of a slightly different design, using a series of rectangles rather than cylinders and without the domed tops. And, of course, none of the East Bay piers was taken to bedrock. Only the two western-most piers involved major caissons; the remainder, which support the truss and viaduct spans, are simple metal or concrete piers on pilings.

The most unusual support on the East Bay was Pier E-9, which linked the truss spans with the viaduct spans. It was built on piles but comprised a square plan with four metal columns. This pier is also set in a bend in the road; it was described at the time as "the longitudinal bracing for the spans approaching the cantilever and stabilizes the curve in the bridge at this point."[6] This four-column design, which joined two very different bridge types and was located at a curve, can in retrospect be seen as the weakest link in the bridge design. The fifty-foot roadway section at E-9 was the only part of the Bay Bridge to fail during the great Loma Prieta earthquake of 1989.

Building the West Bay Superstructure

Contract 6 involved the most closely watched portion of the Bay Bridge project because construction took place within view of the San Francisco waterfront, and because it involved the derring-do of men working high above the water. Look through historic photographs of the Bay Bridge construction and the odds are great that they portray work on Contract 6.

Contract 6 was almost exclusively the work of the U.S. Steel Company and its subsidiaries. The actual contract was awarded to the Columbia Steel Company, a U.S. Steel subsidiary with an office in San Francisco. The metal towers were fabricated by the American Bridge Company and the cables were provided by the American Steel and Wire Company, two more U.S. Steel subsidiaries.

This contract, by far the most expensive of the major contracts, was completed in three steps: building towers of Piers W-2, W-3, and W-4; spinning cable from the San Francisco anchorage to Yerba Buena Island; and installing the stiffening trusses/roadways from San Francisco to the island.

Building the towers, although monumental in scale, was the least complex of the three tasks. Each tower comprises two tall members, called columns, with horizontal and diagonal bracing (or struts) that tie the columns into a unified tower. The columns are about eighty-three feet apart and range in height from 415 feet to 458 feet. Each column is hollow, so designed to enclose a hammerhead derrick. The derrick was used to hoist tower pieces in place, and was raised as the tower was raised. In time, when the tower was complete, the derrick was hoisted out of the column to be reused on another tower.

Cable spinning necessarily awaited completion of the towers and near completion of the anchorages in San Francisco and on

Hammerhead derrick. Courtesy of San Francisco
History Center, San Francisco Public Library.

Yerba Buena Island. By the time the Bay Bridge was constructed,
bridge engineers had nearly a century of experience in doing this
type of work. While it was far from routine—no construction job
thirty to fifty stories off the water can be considered routine—the
cable-spinning procedure was well understood and simply needed
to be carried out in a careful and cautious manner.

The cable spinning comprised at least four major tasks: building a footbridge, called a *catwalk*; spinning wire from one anchorage, over the towers, to the opposite anchorage, and then back
again; compacting the cable; and banding the cable. The catwalk
was a temporary structure, strung on cables the full length of the
West Bay crossing, with a metal flooring and side cable railings.
Simply erecting the catwalk took months but it greatly expedited

a safe and efficient process for spinning the cables. There actually were two catwalks, one for each cable. The photograph here shows workmen attaching cables to the saddle atop one of the towers, while suspended from cranes.

Cable spinning involved unraveling and stretching out miles of 0.19-inch diameter wire across the Bay to the center anchorage and back again, with a parallel process between the center anchorage and Yerba Buena Island. A wheel with wire attached to it was winched along the catwalk, with men stationed at various spots to arrange the wire in strands that would ultimately be bound into cables.

In time the cables were lashed together into great strands and cables that combined the eight major strands. The cables were then fitted with permanent covers, made of impervious steel. These cables were finished in two parts: one from San Francisco to the center pier, which works as a double anchorage; and one from the center pier to Yerba Buena Island.

Catwalk. Courtesy of San Francisco History Center, San Francisco Public Library.

Suspension trusses. Courtesy of San Francisco History Center, San Francisco Public Library.

Hanging the roadway from suspenders off the cables involved a proven technology that was not complicated by the very long length of the suspension spans. When stiffening truss pieces had been hoisted into place, a frame for the roadway was installed at both levels, and from that an asphalt-concrete deck was poured.

Building the East Bay Superstructure

The East Bay crossing work could hardly have been more different from that on the West Bay. U.S. Steel subcontracted much of this work to its competitor Bethlehem Steel. Instead of one single concept and bridge type, the East Bay involved three bridge types: the great 1,400-foot cantilever bridge; a series of through trusses; and a series of double-deck viaducts.

The cantilever bridge was an impressive structure but was dwarfed by the great suspension spans to the west. A cantilever includes three basic elements: the anchor arms, tied to some permanent abutment; the cantilever arms, on the opposite side of the

East Bay cantilever. Courtesy of San Francisco History Center, San Francisco Public Library.

tower that supports the anchor arm; and the clear span, usually much greater than the anchor and cantilever arms put together. For the East Bay, the anchor arms are 608 feet, the cantilever arms 412 feet, and the suspended span is 1,400 feet. Together these lengths approached the record for a cantilever bridge as of 1936.

The anchor arms were built first, with the cantilever arms following. The one innovation was to build the suspended span outward from the cantilever arms, rather than hoisting it into place from the sea level, as had been done in all previous major cantilever bridges. This decision was made by Purcell, who had gained enormous respect for the tidal fluctuations in the Bay and did not want to hinge the fate of the bridge on uncontrollable tidal flows.

Building the Yerba Buena Tunnel

A single contract (Contract 5) was let for all work on Yerba Buena Island, including the anchorage for the West Bay suspension bridge and the abutment and first pier for the East Bay Bridge.

The heart of this contract, however, was the great tunnel through the island, which was, at the time, the largest-diameter tunnel ever built in the world.

Nowhere else in the Bay Area did the Bay Bridge inflict such cataclysmic damage to a natural setting as it did on Yerba Buena Island. The island had been owned by the Navy for about forty years before the bridge was built, but the Navy had trod lightly, causing little permanent damage to the island.

The highway project, however, called for excavating a tunnel seventy-eight feet by fifty-eight feet through the center of the island. The contractor, Clinton Construction, subcontracted with a mining construction company to blast away this tunnel and carry the massive amounts of detritus to some other location. T. E. Connolly, a subcontractor to Clinton Construction, blasted its way through the hillside and removed the debris to a nearby fill site on the north shore of Yerba Buena, where the Army Corps of Engineers planned to create Treasure Island, the proposed site of the upcoming Golden Gate International Exposition and, ultimately, a new Navy station.

The process of rock removal mimicked that of the mining projects with which Connolly was quite familiar. Rock was excavated by the ton and deposited in the shallows or at the north shore. The tunnels were dug from the top down until there was a sizable opening. Concrete was poured in massive amounts to secure the top of the tunnel. The remainder of the tunnel was then excavated to full proportions.

Elsewhere, construction required massive earth-moving to prepare the west slope for the anchorage for the suspension bridge. In retrospect, it is clear that the Bay Bridge ravaged a reasonably intact island in the Bay in ways that would never be acceptable by modern environmental standards.

Building the Bay Bridge from the Perspective of the Workers

More than 8,300 men worked on the Bay Bridge at one time or another, although the peak employment on any given day was about 4,000.[7] These men performed so many tasks as to defy easy categorization; there was no typical experience among them because their jobs were so varied. It is clear, however, that the experiences

Yerba Buena Tunnel. Courtesy of San Francisco History Center, San Francisco Public Library.

were much different for the thousands of employees of the contractors as opposed to the much smaller number of employees of the state.

Contract Employees on the Project

Thanks to the fastidious nature of the Bay Bridge Division resident engineer, I. O. Jahlstrom, we have a remarkably complete record of the men who worked on Contract 2, the substructure for the West Bay crossing. This contract was awarded to the Transbay Construction Company, a single-purpose consortium of companies affiliated with the Six Companies group. The workforce for this contract was not necessarily representative of the workforce for the others, particularly the two high steel contracts. Contract 2 is, however, the one that gives us the most detailed view of the men who built the Bay Bridge.

According to Jahlstrom's notes, the workforce for Contract 2 peaked at 968 men in March 1934 as the job was just ramping up. It held at about that level through January 1935 and then declined rapidly until the contract was completed in June 1935.[8]

Most of these employees were hired by the General Construction Company, which might have handled payroll for the various partner firms. Jahlstrom used March 1934 (the peak of employment) to characterize this workforce. At that time, the vast majority of the workers hailed from the Bay Area. Of 968 men, 896, or 92 percent, came from California, with 849 of those Californians from the Bay Area. The bulk of the rest came from the Pacific Northwest, including Washington State (20), Oregon (11), and Idaho (6); the other men came from various states, with only one, two, or three from each state. Those from the Pacific Northwest likely followed the parent firms, most of which were located in Washington, Idaho, and Oregon.

All were nonunion workers except for those employed in eight unionized crafts: welders, caulkers, hoist operators, boatsmen, structural iron welders, electricians, riggers, and painters. Daily wages ranged from a high of $26.67 to a low of $5.00 per hour. The most common classification was laborer, which earned the lowest ($5.00 per day) wage. There were 453 laborers, more than half of the work force, which explains why the average was close to the lowest wage. The next–most numerous classification was carpenter, a union job, which paid $8.00 per day. The highest-paid workers by far were the divers, who were paid $26.67 per day, followed by foremen, who were paid $13.00 per day. Generally, the men worked thirty hours a week (five six-hour shifts), in response to conditions imposed by the federal loan.

As to the life histories of these men, as noted above we know most were Californians, with 896 of the 968 from the Bay Area, although there were no specific set-asides for local hires. The specifications did award a priority to military veterans, specifically giving prior preferences to veterans with families. Jahlstrom documents that 24.7 percent of workers were veterans. The contracts also specifically forbade hiring from four groups of people: aliens, convicts, Chinese, and Mongolians.[9]

It appears that the situation was a little different for the two high steel contracts: Contract 6 for the West Bay suspension bridge and Contract 7 for the East Bay spans. Contract 6 was a huge job, employing an average of 690 men a day.[10] Similarly large numbers were employed on the East Bay spans. The job classifications for high steel work were dominated by unionized classifications of skilled workers: riggers, rodmen, stationary engineers, and machinists. Workers in these unionized classifications generally commanded more money than the laborers, who dominated the substructure work. Anecdotal information suggests that a higher percentage of high steel workers came from out-of-state as the contractors recruited experienced men who had worked previously on large buildings and bridges in the East and Midwest.

The actual life experiences of these high steel men are captured in a few reminiscences that offer some sense of what these jobs entailed. Peter Stackpole was the son of nationally known sculptor, Ralph Stackpole; Peter would himself become a nationally recognized photographer. As an adventurous young man in his early twenties, Stackpole recorded construction on the high steel spans of the Bay Bridge. He did this as a speculative venture; he was not the official state photographer but was allowed on the job site at the discretion of the resident engineer.[11] During this work Stackpole befriended an experienced high steel man, Joe Walton. Walton was from the East Coast and had worked on the

Empire State Building and the Benjamin Franklin Bridge as well as numerous other high steel jobs. He was broke, and drove to California in the winter of 1934; there he was chagrined to find the steel work would not begin for another two months after his arrival. Fortuitously, he met Jim Ward, a supervisor with the American Bridge Company. Ward knew Walton from several East Coast jobs and loaned him some money while arranging for future work on the bridge. Ward stayed with the Bay Bridge until it was completed before moving to a bridge job in Hartford, Connecticut, where he was killed.

Walton's stories to Stackpole had little to do with the dangers of the work and much more to do with the camaraderie of the workers and their adventurous nightlife in San Francisco. Walton also claimed responsibility for a persistent myth that at least one man was buried in the concrete of the center pier anchorage. He maintains that he and his friends as a prank packed a pair of shoes into the final finished concrete on the anchorage, which left the impression that someone connected to those shoes was buried inside.[12]

Alfred Zampa was another experienced high steel worker who was employed on the Bay Bridge. Unlike Walton, Zampa was a native Californian, having been born in 1905 to Italian immigrant parents in Crockett, near the Carquinez Bridge. He worked at the sugar refinery in Crockett until 1926, when he hired on with the company building the Carquinez Bridge. He enjoyed the high steel work there and spent most of the rest of his life chasing one high steel job after another across the country. In 1934 he returned to the Bay Area to work on the Bay Bridge and later the Golden Gate Bridge. Although he suffered a major injury on the Golden Gate job, he went on to participate in building fifteen major high steel projects. He continued to work in high steel until he was sixty-five. When asked in 1986 to name his favorite among the bridges he worked on, he replied: "My favorite? Bay Bridge. Jesus, look at her. Two suspensions end to end, six different kinds of bridges, 8¼ miles long, deepest piers in the world. We lost 24 men; we'd dangle up there like monkeys driving shot iron. No net. You fell, that was it. They thought we was all crazy."[13]

As an elderly man, Zampa would recall the general character of high steel work, on the Bay Bridge, the Golden Gate Bridge, and elsewhere. In 1986 he told author John Van der Zee that many of the young men hired to work on the two Bay Area bridges found that they could not handle the strain of the acrophobia that would sometimes seize them and leave them immobilized. "People freeze up there. They hang on—they won't fall but it would take three or four of us to break 'em loose. We'd put a line on 'em and let 'em down. They were mostly inexperienced men—they think they can do it but they can't. They say, 'Don't look down.' I never avoided looking down—it didn't bother me. I could look right down in the water and see big fish there. You have to have a little bit of fear—not too much—way back here, in the back of your head. You can't daydream—or you'll take chances."[14]

How often these acrophobic seizures occurred is not stated. Zampa's comments do, however, indicate that building the Bay Bridge was not the ordinary job experience of most Americans of the time.

Zampa's heroism and longevity would culminate in the state of California naming the 2003 Carquinez Bridge, which replaced the bridge where Zampa learned his craft, the Alfred Zampa Memorial Bridge.

State Employees on the Project

California state employees assigned to this job were exposed to many of the same dangers as the contract workers. Dozens of them worked on the bridge. None was killed and only one was seriously injured when he was caught between two barges, which broke both of his legs. Nonetheless, these state workers were there with the contract workers and participated in the same give-and-take of fear and bravado. Arthur Elliott, who would spend his entire career with the state and rise to positions of leadership, came to the Bay Bridge Division as a young graduate of engineering school with no high steel experience. He recalled in 1986,

> I had been a resident engineer on a small bridge in Oregon where the steel trusses were maybe 30 ft. in the air. So I

shall never forget the day I first set foot on the Bay Bridge catwalk and started up toward a tower top and nothing but a little wire mesh and a lot of open air between me and the bay below. The worst aspect was not being able to show any fear. The steelworkers were merciless, and to preserve any self-respect we had to act nonchalant and follow along, walking those beams and planks, climbing through small holes and hanging by our teeth even though our clothes were drenched with cold sweat.[15]

I. O. Jahlstrom also came to the Bay Bridge Division as a resident engineer, to supervise and coordinate construction by the contractors. He was born in Oregon in 1900 and received his degree in civil engineering from Washington State University in 1923. He worked with the Washington State Highway Department for several years before joining the California Division of Highways in 1928. He worked on typical state bridges for several years before joining the Bay Bridge Division in 1933. He was the resident engineer (essentially the state's representative) on two huge contracts: Contract 2, the West Bay substructure; and Contract 6, the West Bay suspension bridge.

In a 1982 oral history Jahlstrom recalled that the Bay Bridge Division hired dozens of temporary and full-time workers who had experience in engineering as well as the industrial and construction crafts. He recalled, "It was the height of the depression. At that time, there were not only unemployed engineers but many men experienced in shop and field inspection and men who had been construction superintendent. We hired these. I had two steel inspectors who came over from England; one became the head inspector."[16]

Jahlstrom, like Elliott, recalled that state workers needed to at least feign the same fearlessness as the contract employees. He recalled one incident:

I remember one man I worked with, Herb Deardorf. He was an inspector of cable and steel work. The first time I got to know about him, they were talking about the time he was celebrating the night after we had finished spinning cables. This fellow was walking down the cables before we had finished the hand line out there. It almost scared me to death. I said I suppose that Herb's up there and they said he'd been a descendent of Daniel Boone. I said he better not try any of this Daniel Boone stuff. I hate to see a man walking on that round cable up there without any hand lines.[17]

Yet another state engineer left his impressions of this work, this time in meter. We know little about Peter Mourer Jr. except that he was a licensed civil engineer, worked for the Bay Bridge Division as a construction engineer, and followed work around California during the post–World War II years. In 1935 he wrote a poem, which the division of highways published in its journal:

How many minds and hands are joined to rear
This towered path across the wind-swept bay!
Men pitied Norton but the engineer
Made his plan a reality. Today
Gaunt towers pierce the foggy shroud of night
And flood-lights gleam on blocks of man-made stone
That bind to rock against the water's might,
An highway, such as gods did never own![18]

Accidents and Death during Construction

As noted earlier, I. O. Jahlstrom, the resident engineer, retained a detailed account of labor conditions on the substructure work for the west crossing, and it is from his records that we derive our clearest images of the dangerous nature of the work there. During the course of this contract, the workmen logged 214,870 man-days.[19] Over that time, 684 men were injured, resulting in the loss of 15,561 man-days. This ratio of man-days lost to total man-days suggests that it was quite likely that any given worker was going to miss a day or more due to injury.

According to Jahlstrom, the 685 serious injuries included five fatalities, 230 accidents resulting in lost time, 322 requiring a doctor's visit but no lost time, and 127 handled through first aid. Jahlstrom even attempted to categorize the serious injuries. Of the 685 accidents, 136 involved men being "crushed or severely bruised," 52 involved strains, and 12 were "objects in eye"; the rest were a variety of less common injuries, including infections and burns.[20]

Unfortunately, we have no such accounting for work on the two high steel contracts, which might have been the most dangerous of all. We do have detailed information about the fatalities for all contracts, in an informative article published by the *San Francisco Chronicle*, as part of a major celebration at the time of the bridge's opening. The newspaper's count totaled twenty-eight fatalities, which does not jibe with the state's record of twenty-four fatalities, a difference likely explained by four deaths that were not treated as construction related. One man died of a heart attack, for example, but his death was not attributed to the working conditions.[21]

The newspaper was able to identify the contracts associated with twenty-four of these deaths. Contract 7 (the high steel for the East Bay) accounted for six deaths, while Contract 6 (the suspension span high steel work) involved only four deaths. The West Bay substructure resulted in five deaths. The remaining fatalities were scattered among the other contracts.

The cause of death was identified for twenty-four of the fatalities. Not surprisingly, falling was the leading cause, resulting in fifteen (more than 60 percent) of the fatalities. Several men were crushed by machinery or hit in the head by falling bolts and other metal objects.

Bay Bridge Workers and the General Strike of 1934

Although there were only limited labor problems involving the Bay Bridge Division and its contractors, work on the Bay Bridge was profoundly affected by the great San Francisco general strike in the summer of 1934. The strike had little to do with Bay Bridge issues but was particularly important to the project because the West Bay substructure work and San Francisco anchorage work were just getting under way at the time of the strike. These two contracts were also greatly affected by the fact that much of the Bloody Thursday violence, the most intense event of the long general strike, occurred July 5, 1934, on Rincon Hill, where the San Francisco Anchorage was under construction.

Purcell ordered all Bay Bridge work to cease the day after Bloody Thursday. Governor Frank Merriam announced the halt:

I have been informed by Charles H. Purcell that all construction on the San Francisco–Oakland Bay Bridge has been abandoned due to strikers' battles with police. Early this morning the hauling of dirt from excavations for the bridge viaduct on Rincon Hill…was discontinued because of the intimidation of the strikers. Rock throwing and violence drove off the 100 men of the Healy–Tibbitts Construction Company at 9:50 AM. At 10:00 AM conditions forced the State bridge engineers, supervising the work, to flee from the job. The strikers are occupying Rincon Hill, armed with rocks and clubs, and have driven the viaduct construction workmen from the spot. [22]

I. O. Jahlstrom, ever the most-reliable chronicler of the construction job, reported that 3,700 of 4,000 people working on the Bay Bridge were out of work during the last half of July 1934. He noted that on Contract 2, few workers were unionized but the specialized union jobs were too crucial to do without. In any event, he noted, "Policy would have demanded suspension in any case, considering the hazards from possible sabotage and risks that nonunion men would have taken running the gauntlet to and from the site."[23]

Work was discontinued, all or in part, until July 22, a closure of nearly three weeks. Despite this setback, the bridge was completed shortly ahead of schedule, a little more than two years after Bloody Thursday.

Notes

1. Contract 1, for Bay foundation testing, had already been completed by 1933.

2. California Department of Public Works, "First Annual Progress Report, San Francisco–Oakland Bay Bridge," July 1, 1934.

3. The history of building the bridge is indebted to I.O. Jahlstrom, the resident engineer for this contract who kept copious notes about all aspects of the job. His notes are stored in the Transportation Library of Caltrans in Sacramento.

4. Carlton S. Proctor, "Foundation Design for the Trans-Bay Bridge," *Civil Engineering* 4, no. 12 (December 1934): 617–21. See also other articles throughout the 1930s.

5. A clamshell bucket is a dredging devise, hinged at the top, roughly in the shape of a clamshell.

6. V. A. Endersby, "Final Construction Report of the Substructure, East Bay Crossing, San Francisco–Oakland Bay Bridge Contract 4 and 4a," July 28, 1937.

7. There were no women among the workers.

8. This section comes from I. O. Jahlstrom, "General Construction Report for Foundations, Piers 2, 3, 4, 5, 6 and 24 of Contract No. 2 for the West Bay Crossing of the San Francisco–Oakland Bay Bridge," February 27, 1937.

9. Jahlstrom was resident engineer on other contracts as well and in each case he repeated the hiring prohibitions: "No Chinese or Mongolian labor shall be employed. No convict labor shall be employed." With respect to aliens, the contracts specified a fine of $10.00 per day per alien. Alien in this usage refers to non-citizens.

10. I. O. Jahlstrom, "General Construction report for the Superstructure for the West Bay Crossing of the San Francisco–Oakland Bay Bridge," May 1, 1937. Unfortunately, Jahlstrom was not as careful in documenting the workforce for this contract.

11. Peter Stackpole, *The Bridge Builders* (San Francisco, CA: Pomegranate Artbooks, 1984). Stackpole's bridge pictures are part of the permanent collection of the Oakland Museum.

12. Ibid., 24. This myth gained some traction but is not supported by the facts. Two men died in building the center pier/anchorage: one from a heart attack, the other from a fall to the water outside the pier.

13. "He Built Them All, Great and Small," *San Francisco Chronicle*, November 4, 1986, 4.

14. Van der Zee, *The Gate*, 258.

15. Arthur L. Elliott, "High Level Engineering," *Civil Engineering* (October 1986).

16. "Highway Recollections of I. O. Jahlstrom," California Department of Transportation Library, Sacramento, 14.

17. Jahlstrom, "General Construction Report for Foundations, Piers 2, 3, 4, 5, 6 and 24 of Contract No. 2 for the West Bay Crossing of the San Francisco–Oakland Bay Bridge," 16.

18. *California Highways and Public Works*, February 1935, 21.

19. A man-day is defined as one man working one day.

20. Jahlstrom, "General Construction Report for Foundations, Piers 2, 3, 4, 5, 6 and 24 of Contract No. 2 for the West Bay Crossing of the San Francisco–Oakland Bay Bridge," 167.

21. "Another Honor Roll," *San Francisco Chronicle*, November 12, 1936.

22. "The Darkest Day in San Francisco since the 1906 Earthquake,"*San Francisco Chronicle*, July 6, 1934.

23. Jahlstrom, "General Construction Report for Foundations, Piers 2, 3, 4, 5, 6 and 24 of Contract No. 2 for the West Bay Crossing of the San Francisco–Oakland Bay Bridge," 171.

CHAPTER 7

What Happened to the Bay Bridge

From 1936 to the 1989 Loma Prieta Earthquake

For the most part, the Bay Bridge had an uneventful history between its completion in 1936 and the Loma Prieta earthquake of 1989. The long trend over time was a relentless increase in usage, until the average daily traffic was nearly three times what the planners had originally forecast. Four major developments stand out within the otherwise routine life story of this bridge: the Golden Gate International Exposition, 1939–40; planning for the Southern Crossing Bridge, in the 1940s and 1950s; the reconstruction of the Bay Bridge, 1958–63; and, of course, the Loma Prieta earthquake of 1989.

Golden Gate International Exposition, 1939–40

The Golden Gate International Exposition was initially planned as a celebration of the completion of the Golden Gate and Bay Bridges. Planning for the festivity lagged for a few years, however, just long enough for the attention of the people of the Bay Area to shift from celebrating the bridges to worrying about the wars that were developing in Asia and Europe. In the end, the exposition was a world's fair that occurred near the center of the Bay Bridge and that had considerable impact on the operations of the bridge during its early years.

The Bay Bridge had not been designed with a World's Fair in mind and access from the bridge to the exposition was awkward at best. Ideally, mass transit would have served the event. There was very little parking on either Treasure Island or Yerba Buena Island, and Treasure Island (the site of the fair) was connected to Yerba Buena Island and the Bay Bridge by a somewhat narrow causeway and circuitous ramps from the bridge. The railways, however, were no more designed to serve the Golden Gate

109

Golden Gate International Exposition. Courtesy of San Francisco History Center, San Francisco Public Library.

International Exposition than were the automobile aspects of the bridge. The railways could stop at Yerba Buena Island, but that was still more than a mile from the exposition, an unacceptably long distance for moving large crowds.

In time, the division of highways and the Key System decided to rely on two modes of transportation to satisfy the demand: one old mode, ferries; and one emerging mode, bus transportation. The division of highways did not provide bus service but reoriented its roadways leading to Treasure Island to accommodate buses as well as the trucks that served the concessions. The Key System in 1939 temporarily reopened its Key System Mole to take trains to the middle of the Bay and allow ferries to complete the trip from the East Bay to the fair. In 1940 the Key System changed course and moved its ferry boats to provide service between San Francisco and Treasure Island, while relying on buses to link the East Bay with the exposition.[1]

The Golden Gate International Exposition proved little about the operations of the Bay Bridge except to foretell the kind of traffic jams that would burden it, almost from the day it opened, and would lead to persistent attempts to increase its capacity.

Planning for the Southern Crossing Bridge

During the 1940s and early 1950s, a variety of factors conspired to diminish the ability of the Bay Bridge to operate as it had been designed. Among these were the military buildup before, during, and just after World War II, including massive activities by military contractors; the decline of the interurbans; the construction of freeways on both sides of the Bay; and the general dispersal of populations around the Bay Area. These developments were all interrelated. The decision to build freeways, for example, was prompted in part by the great military buildup. Freeways in turn facilitated a dispersal of Bay Area population down the Peninsula from San Francisco and south along the Eastshore Freeway below Oakland. The interurbans failed, in part because of bad management but also because the freeways offered a much faster way to get around. All of these trends created huge backlogs on the automobile lanes on the upper deck of the Bay Bridge. As this congestion got worse with each passing year, one popular solution called for construction of another bridge to the south, commonly called the Southern Crossing Bridge.

The proposal to build a southern crossing (roughly between Hunters Point in San Francisco and the southern tip of Alameda Island) hinged on resolution of two additional matters: What should the State of California do with the Bay Bridge if the interurbans were to fail? And how could local or state government provide some new type of transbay mass transit if the interurbans were to fail? The southern crossing was debated for decades—it has its supporters even today—but momentum for its construction effectively died in 1958, when the interurban cars and tracks were removed from the lower deck of the Bay Bridge to make way for additional automobile lanes.

The War Department initiated studies for a southern crossing just prior to American entry into World War II, as the massive prewar buildup by the Navy and Army threatened to choke city streets around and near military bases. The Navy in particular was beefing up its presence south of the Bay Bridge, with a major facility at Hunters Point, a large supply station in Oakland, and Naval Air Station, Alameda, a substantial naval air station. Concerned about impacts to local streets, Congress directed a joint Army–Navy board to study the need for and feasibility of the federal government building a bridge between Hunters Point and Bay Farm Island in Alameda.[2] The board reported in November 1941, however, that such a crossing was not justified for national defense purposes.

Automobile traffic actually abated slightly during the war due to gasoline and rubber rationing, only to skyrocket in the immediate postwar period. In 1945 and 1946 Congress and the California legislature mandated studies of new bridges by a second joint Army–Navy board and by the California Department of Public Works. The two resulting studies went in opposing directions. The state agency in 1947 came out in favor of a new high steel bridge just north of the Bay Bridge, reusing old Bay Bridge plans whenever possible. The Army–Navy board recommended a southern crossing.[3]

With some Bay Area leaders favoring the high bridge and others the southern crossing, conflict tore apart the consensus that had been so crucial in getting the Bay Bridge built. San Francisco officials favored the southern crossing, whereas East Bay leaders leaned toward the high steel solution.

One unexpected product of this debate was a bridge design (the Butterfly design) developed by Frank Lloyd Wright for the southern crossing. Wright supported the southern crossing, believing that the location lent itself to a quieter, less muscular bridge. His proposed bridge was strictly a Taliesin project, not funded or endorsed by any official party, and comprised a reinforced concrete viaduct with a double arch in the center to provide for a shipping channel two thousand feet wide and two hundred feet tall. The north and southbound lanes were separated, held together by a suspended garden and walkway structure.[4]

What ultimately killed consideration of Wright's and all other proposals for a southern crossing was the momentous decision by the interurbans to abandon service on the Bay Bridge.

When the rails were removed, vehicular capacity almost immediately increased by 25 percent. The removal of the interurban tracks did not, of course, solve the long-term problem of moving people from the East Bay to San Francisco. It simply shifted that traffic from rail cars into automobiles and buses. It did, however, completely deflate any momentum for the southern crossing, although, as noted, that bridge alignment still has a few major supporters, even today.

Reconstruction of the Bay Bridge, 1958–63

The Key System, the last active interurban using the Bay Bridge, petitioned to abandon its line in 1955.[5] In 1956 the CTBA ordered its staff to begin studying how best to use the southern half of the lower deck of the bridge, which housed the soon-to-be-abandoned rails. In 1957 the legislature authorized funds for that study, and later that year authorized the work itself.

At first glance the adaptation of the bridge to convert rail to highway uses should have involved nothing more than paving over the rail lanes. In actual practice, the conversion required reconstructing many aspects of the upper and lower decks because each had been built to a specific standard as to height, load, and lane width. Converting this triple purpose (car, train, and truck) bridge to a single general utility required a complete makeover that required three years, which is as long as it took to build the bridge in the first place.

To recapitulate the original design, the Bay Bridge was built to handle six lanes of automobile traffic on the top deck, three in each direction. The bottom deck was designed to handle three lanes of truck traffic and two sets of transit rails. This design both hampered and facilitated the reuse of the bridge without rail traffic. The good news was that the bridge as a whole was engineered to include rail traffic, the heaviest loading for the structure. This meant that, by removing the weighty rails and the even weightier rail cars, the total load for the bridge would decrease with reconstruction. The bad news was that the upper deck was designed for automobiles only, meaning it would need to be reinforced before heavier trucks and buses could be accepted there. It meant as well that the Yerba Buena Island Tunnel would need to be reconfigured to allow tall trucks and buses to pass through an upper level designed for cars only.

There was also a huge problem in San Francisco, where the approach spans were designed with a specific purpose in mind: cars on the upper deck, trucks and trains on the lower deck. The conversion of the San Francisco approaches was arguably the most complicated aspect of the 1958 reconstruction and it affected all aspects of the plans for the late 1950s work. For example, at a basic level, the upper deck cars traveled on different ramps, depending on whether they were going to or returning from the East Bay. Putting all eastbound traffic on the same level required repurposing on-ramps as off-ramps, and vice versa. The situation was even more complicated in dealing with the old truck and train on and off ramps, which needed to be totally repurposed on the San Francisco side and, to a lesser degree, on the Oakland side. So profound was the need for reconfiguring the San Francisco approaches that this task governed the decision as to which level would be westbound and which would be eastbound. The division of highways determined that it would be much simpler to redo the San Francisco approaches if the top deck became the westbound span. That decision, in turn, governed all other aspects of the redesign.

In the first phase of work in 1960, the San Francisco approaches were reconstructed or newly constructed, the upper deck was strengthened to accommodate truck and bus traffic, and the rail section of the lower deck was paved over.[6] The second phase, which took place in 1961, involved rebuilding the Yerba Buena Island Tunnel and viaducts while strengthening the upper deck. To accomplish this without closing the bridge, the division of highways built a temporary bridge that allowed work to go on while keeping half the tunnel open to traffic. During the final phase, accomplished in 1962 and 1963, workers strengthened the upper deck on the East Bay crossing, and added new lightweight pavement. The reconstructed decks were opened to unidirectional traffic on October 12, 1963.[7]

The restructure of the Bay Bridge between 1958 and 1963 changed the look as well as the functioning of the structure. Although the bridge retained its essential appearance, the

alterations brought the structure into the modern postwar function. No longer was it a quaint multipurpose structure with trains
and trucks segregated from automobiles. By 1963 the Bay Bridge
was a modernized part of the interstate highway system, carrying I-80 to its western terminus and linking the extensive freeway
system on the peninsula with the even more extensive freeway
network in the East Bay.

The Loma Prieta Earthquake, 1989

The Bay Bridge remained unchanged structurally between completion of the reconstruction in 1963 and the massive Loma Prieta
Earthquake in 1989. During that quarter century the bridge served
in its new vehicular-only capacity, while much of the rest of the
Bay Area transportation network evolved quickly. The Bay Bridge
arguably became less important during those years because transportation options multiplied through construction of the BART
system, the Peninsula Commute Service (Caltrain) system, and
new light rail lines in Santa Clara County, along with huge freeway extensions, including I-280 down the Peninsula. In no sense,
however, did the bridge fade into insignificance. It was by far the
busiest structure in the area and the key link between the East Bay
and San Francisco. At the time of its reconstruction, the bridge
was handling about 110,000 cars a day; it was handling about
240,000 cars on the day of the Loma Prieta earthquake.

The importance of the bridge and its capacity became dramatically apparent late in the day on October 17, 1989. Fortuitously,
the afternoon rush hour traffic was lighter than usual that day, a
happy circumstance that is generally attributed to the fact that the
third game of the 1989 World Series was set to begin at 5:30 PM
at Candlestick Park in San Francisco, a game involving the two
Bay Area professional baseball teams, the San Francisco Giants
and the Oakland Athletics. Traffic eastbound was moving at an
average speed of forty-eight miles per hour while westbound
was moving at fifty-four miles per hour when the earth suddenly
shook at 5:04 PM.[8]

The California Highway Patrol later attempted to recon-
struct the series of events that occurred just after the earthquake
struck. A high percentage of drivers said they were listening to the

pregame coverage from Candlestick Park on their car radios and first recognized there was a problem when the broadcasters went off the air. The physical sensation of the quake differed on the various sections of the bridge. Drivers in the tunnel felt nothing but knew something was wrong when the tunnel lights went out. Motorists on the suspension span felt a side-to-side movement while those on the through truss spans felt a violent jolt. Luckily, most drivers slowed down instinctively, and there were surprisingly few accidents attributable to the earthquake.

The quake caused little direct damage to the bridge except at Pier E-9, the juncture of the through truss section and the continuous deck trusses, located about halfway between Yerba Buena Island and the Oakland touchdown. This pier is unique among Bay Bridge piers in that it includes a four-column box that joins two different structure types, with fifty-foot-long metal roadway sections on both levels. The quake caused the through truss and deck truss sections to move in different ways. The continuous truss was thought to have moved 5.5 inches to the east, away from the pier. Both fifty-foot roadway sections fell. It is likely that the top deck fell first and took out the lower deck with it. The sections remained attached to the west but ramped downward on the east.

Relatively few vehicles were on these roadway sections at the time they failed. One automobile was traveling westbound on the upper deck when it collapsed. The driver had come to a complete stop in response to the motion of the quake. When the top deck fell, the automobile went with it, ramping downward until it was wedged against the lower deck. The driver and his passenger crawled out through a car window and walked back to Oakland. Both were seriously injured and the car was totaled. Meanwhile, a motorcyclist traveling eastbound at a high rate of speed just missed going over the brink created by the failure of the lower deck. He was able to stop, turn around, and return to San Francisco. An eastbound commuter van carrying thirteen people when the top deck collapsed escaped with little damage to the vehicle or passengers.

The lone fatality on the Bay Bridge occurred as the panicked drivers of hundreds of vehicles attempted to find a way off the structure. There were no police on the bridge at the time but

Failure at Pier E-9. Courtesy of Joe Lewis.

volunteers—a Caltrans worker, sailors from the Treasure Island Naval Station, and concerned civilians—staged an orderly evacuation for nearly all the stranded drivers. Motorists westbound on the upper deck but east of Pier E-9 simply turned around and returned to Oakland, driving the wrong way. Eastbound traffic east of the break simply continued on its way to Oakland. The biggest problem was for traffic going eastbound, especially those stuck between Yerba Buena Island and the break at Pier E-9. These drivers could not proceed to Oakland because of the break and could hardly return to San Francisco because of the miles of stalled eastbound cars that needed to turn around and somehow get back to San Francisco.

The lone fatality was a female driver, Anamafi Moala Kalushia, who, with her brother, were just east of Yerba Island when the E-9 decks collapsed. Traffic came to a sudden and complete stop. A Caltrans worker, acting as traffic cop, suggested she turn around, take an exit at Yerba Buena Island, go to the upper deck, and return to San Francisco. For unknown reasons, the driver ignored this advice and continued driving toward Oakland—and the break—at a high rate of speed. Her car went airborne for about forty feet at the E-9 break before it struck the collapsed upper deck. The driver died instantly; her brother survived.[9]

The broken bridge was closed for one month and one day, until Caltrans could cut away the damaged roadway segments, install I-beams to span the missing fifty-foot section, and install precast concrete roadways on the I-beams.

Notes

1. Demoro, *The Key System*, 101–2.

2. Division of San Francisco Bay Toll Crossings, "Southern Crossing of San Francisco Bay," December 1955.

3. David W. Jones, "California's Freeway Era in Historical Perspective," July 1989, Institute of Transportation Studies, University of California–Berkeley.

4. "Bridge the Bay: Unbuilt Projects," U.C. Berkeley Library, 1999. Wright's design would be resurrected when the East Bay crossing was studied for replacement.

5. The cause of the failure of the interurbans goes far beyond the scope of this book. It is analyzed in great detail in Seymour Adler, *The Political Economy of Transit in the San Francisco Bay Area, 1945–1963* (Berkeley, CA: Institute of Urban and Regional Development, 1989). The failure of the interurbans also led to discussions of how to replace them, discussions that would culminate in construction of the Bay Area Rapid Transit, or BART system.

6. This work is summarized in a series of articles by the chief engineer, N. C. Raab, in *California Highways and Public Works* in 1960.

7. E. R. Foley, "Bay Bridge Reconstruction," *California Highways and Public Works* (March–April 1964).

8. Department of California Highway Patrol, "1989 Loma Prieta Earthquake Summary Report," 1989, 4.

9. Ibid., 10.

CHAPTER 8

A Repair Effort Becomes a Megaproject

The Decision to Replace the East Span of the Bay Bridge

In the immediate aftermath of the Loma Prieta earthquake, the primary focus of transportation planners throughout California was on double-deck concrete viaducts, similar to the Cypress Street Viaduct in Oakland that had completely collapsed and that resulted in significant loss of life. Sixty-two people died during the Loma Prieta earthquake, forty-two of them on the Cypress Street Viaduct. It was obvious to all that this double-deck design, particularly when built on fill, had been a terrible mistake. First attention after 1989 was directed to rebuilding the Cypress in a safer configuration, replacing or massively reinforcing any viaducts of a similar design, and dealing with any other concrete structures with columns unable to withstand seismic movement. The Bay Bridge, where a single person died and the structure was back in service in about a month, was the least of their concerns.

In the early post-earthquake analyses, little attention was paid to the Bay Bridge because it had not failed in a huge way and because the fixes for its weaknesses were so simple and inexpensive. As one example of the analysis of the Bay Bridge by the engineering community in the immediate post-earthquake environment, the National Institute of Standards and Technology (NIST), a research arm of the U.S. Department of Commerce, in 1990 published "Performance of Structures during the Loma Prieta Earthquake of October 17, 1989."[1] The report focused on the failure of buildings, particularly in the Marina District of San Francisco, and of bridges, especially the Cypress Street Viaduct in Oakland. The study included an eleven-page analysis of the performance of the Bay Bridge. The conclusions of that section were as follows:

1. Damage to the San Francisco–Oakland Bay Bridge was concentrated within three general areas. These included the

119

collapse of the upper and lower link spans at Pier E-9 and the shearing of the truss shoe retainer bolts for spans between E-17 and E-23; and the near loss of spans E-23/E-24.

2. In general, the entire structure performed remarkably well and what damage there was proved to be minor. It may be useful, however, to conduct a detailed investigation of the subsoil conditions, particularly beneath the East Bay spans, characterize their dynamic properties, and then use this as a set of boundary conditions for a full three-dimensional transient dynamics analysis of the complete section from Yerba Buena Island to Pier 23 to arrive at anticipated maximum displacement demand at the truss shoe connections. These data would then permit better design of the shoe size as well as the required strength of the restraining bolts.[2]

The NIST focused on what had worked and what had failed during the earthquake. For the viaducts, the failure was obvious and catastrophic. For the Bay Bridge, the failure was minor and isolated to the truss shoe connections and other linkages. Recommendations related to how to fix the identified problems.

An early official study by the state of California drew similar conclusions regarding the severity of the problems with the Bay Bridge. In 1990 a panel of distinguished scientists and engineers appointed by Governor George Deukmejian released its report on damage from the Loma Prieta earthquake and the state of the state's seismic retrofit program.[3] The board, called a board of inquiry, made nine "Findings on Bay Bridge Span Failure."

1. The E-9 spans fell when bolted connections were sheared at the truss shoes, allowing the deck segment to shift to the east and fall off the support beams at the west end.
2. The bridge was designed for a 10 percent earthquake acceleration.
3. "The bridge appears to have no design or construction deficiencies" and "there is no indication of subsequent maintenance deficiencies" that could have contributed to the failure.
4. Caltrans had not identified the Bay Bridge as being vulnerable.
5. There was "no evidence that foundation failure contributed" to the collapse of Pier E-9.

6. The truss to pier connections at E-9 needed to be studied.
7. The repairs made by Caltrans "appear to be appropriate for the short-term."
8. The board recommended a "dynamic performance" analysis of the bridge.
9. "The Bay Bridge may not be presumed to be adequately earthquake resistant just because it was only slightly damaged during the Loma Prieta earthquake and has since been repaired."[4]

In 1990 the governor created the Seismic Advisory Board (SAB) to advise Caltrans on priorities for seismic safety in its bridge program.[5] Drawing on the advice of the SAB and the earlier board of inquiry report, Caltrans directed most of its efforts in the early 1990s to retrofitting concrete bridge and viaduct columns, which existed by the thousands on the state highway system. The urgency in this regard only increased following the 1994 Northridge earthquake in Southern California, which resulted in the collapse of many more freeway structures, most of them concrete or with concrete columns. For about a decade Caltrans' principal response to both the Loma Prieta and Northridge earthquakes was a massive seismic retrofit program in which thousands of state-owned bridges were fitted with various seismic restraint devices.[6] Most of this work was completed during the 1990s. The effort since the 1990s has focused on retrofitting vulnerable bridges owned by California cities and counties.

Although later analyses would emphasize the dangers to the public of keeping the 1936 Bay Bridge in place, there was very little in the analyses conducted during the immediate post-earthquake period that made such a suggestion. Instead, the bulk of attention in these early years was focused on retrofitting single- and double-column freeway structures, the kind of structures that failed dramatically in both the Loma Prieta and Northridge earthquakes and that accounted for a high percentage of the lives lost.

Study of Retrofit, 1990–93

In the early 1990s Caltrans, having set in motion its massive one- and two-column bridge retrofit program, began to study what should be done with the Bay Bridge and other long toll bridges in the Bay Area. In 1990 Caltrans contracted with Abolhassan Astaneh-Asl, a professor of civil engineering at the University of California–Berkeley to study how the existing Bay Bridge should be retrofitted. The professor issued the first draft of his report in early 1992 and completed the study later that year.[7] The report concluded that a retrofit could be accomplished safely and could be done for about $150 million to $200 million.

Professor Astaneh-Asl recommended fixing the problems that were identified by the NIST and the board of inquiry: the shearing of the restraining bolts for the truss shoes during the earthquake along with other concerns having to do with truss-to-pier connectors. His solution addressed those problems as well as other incidental repairs he deemed necessary.

Between 1990 and 1997 Caltrans debated whether to simply retrofit the bridge at the East Bay crossing or replace it entirely with a new span. The estimated cost for retrofit depended on the evaluation of what it would take to make the existing bridge safe. Professor Astaneh-Asl proposed fixing what was demonstrably wrong with the bridge. His estimate of a $150 million to $200 million fix was proportional to the amount of work contemplated. In the next few years, Caltrans would propose retrofit work thought to cost more than $1 billion, more than five times what Astaneh-Asl proposed. The dramatic difference in cost did not indicate that either Astaneh-Asl or Caltrans was unable to estimate cost for a set level of work. Rather, the difference had to do with what is often called *scope creep*, with Caltrans proposing levels of retrofit work that far exceeded what had been contemplated in the initial years following the Loma Prieta earthquake.

Scope Creep and the Decision for Replacement, 1994–97

Step by step, Caltrans officials and major leaders in California state government between 1994 and 1997 began to move from an earlier assumption that the East Bay spans could be repaired and retrofitted to consideration of, and finally approval for, a replacement alternative. Exactly how and why this shift took place is not well known. It appears that the decision for replacement first took hold among Caltrans officials and spread slowly among elected officials, based on analyses and recommendations from Caltrans and consultants hired by Caltrans.

At its heart, the scope creep for retrofit of the Bay Bridge had to do with adoption by Caltrans of a lifeline status for the Bay Bridge, as well as a few other Bay Area bridges. It is not clear when the agency first began to use this concept but by the mid-1990s the term was commonly used to describe the agency's approach to retrofit of the East Span.

As used by Caltrans, the term *lifeline* referred both to the functional importance of the bridge as well as to standards for retrofit. The first usage backs up a common sense understanding that the Bay Bridge, which carries 250,000 vehicles a day, is central to the economy of the region. Caltrans went so far as to adopt formal criteria for a functioning lifeline structure:

- It allows emergency relief access to and through the affected region.
- It connects major population centers within the affected region.
- It serves as the most effective of several routes for emergency relief access.
- It provides direct or nearby access to and from major emergency supply centers.
- It links various modes of transportation.
- It provides access to major traffic distribution centers.[8]

Caltrans went further to establish a set of standards for retrofitting a lifeline structure, defined in terms of the maximum credible earthquake and duration in which the bridge could be out of service. For the Bay Bridge analyses the maximum credible earthquake was determined to be an earthquake of 8.0 Richter on the San Andreas Fault or a 7.25 Richter on the Hayward Fault.[9] The standard for stability was that the structure would be out of service for no more than a day following a maximum credible earthquake event.

Because the decision to pursue a lifeline status was internal to the agency, there is little public record showing why Caltrans shifted its strategy so dramatically. The rationale for replacement was finally made public in a 2000 publication, *Replacement vs. Retrofit*.[10] By that time, however, the department had already decided on the replacement alternative, having proven to its own satisfaction that the replacement and retrofit costs were comparable and that the new bridge could be built without major difficulties.

The department first hinted publicly that it was seriously exploring a replacement option in its January 1996 report to the legislature on its seismic program. The report indicated, "The Department is exploring the cost effectiveness of an option to build a replacement structure.... At some point it may become both cost effective and efficient to have a modern bridge, fully designed and built to the best standards rather than a bridge with a patchwork of retrofits."[11]

For the remainder of 1996 Caltrans undertook three key studies, which together made a case that the costs for replacement and retrofit were comparable and that replacement was actually cheaper if lifecycle costs, including long-term maintenance, were included. These three studies included an internal analysis of replacement costs for various bridge types, prepared by Caltrans' Office of Structure Design; an external study of replacement versus retrofit costs undertaken by a consulting firm, Ventry Engineering; and a study prepared by Brian Maroney of Caltrans, recapitulating cost estimates for the replacement and retrofit options.[12]

The study by the Office of Structure Design sought to identify the bridge types that would be appropriate as replacement structures and to estimate their costs. The study examined seven alternatives, from a viaduct-only design (what would be called the Skyway alternative in later discussions), to a viaduct with a shipping channel main span just east of Yerba Buena Island (at the approximate location of the 1936 cantilever span) that included either a cable-stayed or a suspension span.[13]

The report addressed directly two issues that would dominate discussions of the East Bay span for more than a decade: the aesthetics and the cost of a replacement structure. The Office of Structure Design was sympathetic to the importance of aesthetics in designing a new Bay crossing: "Given the location of this bridge, aesthetics must be respected in the consideration of type selection. A cable-stayed bridge has been identified as an appropriate candidate for this site. Alignment selection can be recognized coupled with type selection to allow greater opportunity to view the cable-stayed portion of the bridge."[14]

At this point, the Office of Structure Design was recommending a replacement bridge that differed little from what would actually be built. Substitute the cable-stayed main span for the SAS span that was built and the design analyzed in 1996 was fundamentally the same as the design completed in 2013. What was different was the cost. In 1996 the office estimated the replacement bridge would run between $0.9 billion and $1.4 billion, the difference reflecting the cost of the more-expensive main span. With these estimates, even the more dramatic cable-stayed bridge was within the ballpark of the retrofit option, although the Office of Structure Design did not directly estimate the retrofit cost.

A direct comparison of replacement and retrofit did appear in the study by Ventry Engineering, a Florida-based engineering firm specializing in value engineering. Value engineering is a term of art and law in the engineering and construction trades. Under guidelines of the Federal Highway Administration, value engineering is required for all very large projects that might use federal aid. The choice of a Florida-based firm was consistent with federal guidelines, which require value engineering to be conducted by a firm or body not involved, and not likely to be involved, with the ultimate project.[15]

For the sake of analysis, Ventry assumed a bridge similar to the one recommended by the Office of Structure Design: a concrete viaduct with a cable-stayed main span. It also recommended inclusion of bicycle lanes. In general terms, the bridge analyzed by Ventry was quite similar to what was actually built, with the exception being the SAS main span. Ventry estimated the cost of the bridge with bicycle lanes and a tow truck facility at $842 million, or $795 million without the bicycle lanes or tow facility.[16] By contrast, the retrofit was estimated to cost $842 million. If life-cycle costs were factored in, the replacement bridge was estimated to cost $1.13 billion over twenty-five years (less for the stripped-down version), and $1.227 billion for the retrofit.[17]

The Ventry study was presented to the SAB, although it had not yet been vetted through the ordinary document approval process at Caltrans. In early January 1997, the Ventry report was released to the press on the same day that the SAB officially moved to support a replacement bridge over a retrofit project. The simultaneous release of these two scientific studies had enormous influence on local decision-makers, who had previously been on the fence about this subject. The *Contra Costa Times*, for example, used the data from the Ventry study and the SAB motion to opine, "Pursue a new bridge: it's economical, safer, better. What's not to like?" On all the three points, the newspaper reflected the opinions expressed in the Ventry report and the SAB motion (which itself was based generally on the Ventry report).[18] The *Oakland Tribune* reported, "Key Bay Area lawmakers, buoyed by two confidential Caltrans reports, say replacing the Oakland portion of the 60-year-old Bay Bridge now looks like the best option."[19] The two confidential reports were the Ventry study and the action of the SAB.

Clearly, the Office of Structure Design and Ventry Engineering believed that the cost of retrofit and replacement were close to one another. Ventry went so far as to conclude retrofit was more expensive that the proposed replacement, even with a signature span at the shipping channel. This analysis hinged on two important calculations: the cost of the new bridge, and assumptions about what would be required to retrofit the old bridge.

In retrospect one can make three observations. First, the estimated cost for retrofit was rising exponentially with each study. Second, the projected cost for the replacement structure got smaller with each new estimate, although not nearly as quickly as the increase in the estimates for retrofit. Third, the estimate for the new bridge was below the true mark by a factor of more than six.

The actual cost of fully retrofitting the bridge will never be known because that option was never pursued. It is clear, however, that the University of California–Berkeley studies in 1990–92 and the Caltrans studies in 1996–97 were based on widely divergent strategies. The 1990–92 studies focused on truss-to-pier connections. The Caltrans plans, which were advanced to a 65 percent completion, pursued a strategy to "strengthen the foundation (piles and pile cap connections), stiffen the towers, isolate the superstructure and strengthen many superstructure members."[20]

This succinct statement of the retrofit option points out the areas in which the 1996–97 strategy went beyond what was proposed by University of California–Berkeley: strengthening the foundations, stiffening the towers, and strengthening the superstructure elements. The differences were most readily apparent in dealing with the foundation and piers. The earlier studies had presumed the piers and pilings would be left alone. The 1996–97 studies assumed the need to drive new concrete piles.[21] The most dramatic visual impact from this retrofit would have come from the effort to stiffen the towers. The 1996–97 studies assumed that it was necessary to encase all steel towers and piers in concrete, essentially transforming these lattice steel structures into concrete towers. The 1996–97 studies also assumed the need to remove the metal piers below the cantilever spans and replace them with all-concrete structures. In terms of stiffening the superstructure, these studies assumed it was necessary to install an entirely new set of trusses outside the edges of the cantilever spans, greatly increasing the dead load but stiffening the structure. These and other massive changes to the retrofit strategy accounted for the fact that retrofit estimates quintupled between 1992 and 1997. Professor Astaneh-Asl pointed to this fact, noting that it was totally unfair to compare his $150 million to $200 million estimate to what Caltrans was proposing. "Those initial estimates [$150 million to $200 million] were good educated guesses," Astaneh-Asl stated. "But from a policy standpoint, not a research and engineering standpoint, what's evolved is that the Bay Bridge has been held to another standard. It's not good enough now for it just to be safe during an earthquake. It has to be completely up and functional all 10 lanes, immediately."[22]

Karen Frick agrees with Astaneh-Asl that adherence to stringent lifeline stands was ultimately what drove Caltrans to move from a manageable repair project to a commitment to a megaproject:

> The Bay Bridge East Span project, as originally conceived by Caltrans between 1989 and 1996, was never intended to be a megaproject. Caltrans's mission was to engage in a straightforward, albeit technically challenging retrofit project. However, the East Span retrofit spiraled into a colossal undertaking as Caltrans undertook several studies and learned of the technical complexities associated with the bridge and attempted to adhere to the stringent seismic safety standards it had established.

Some observers have questioned whether the level of rigour on the seismic standards, namely adherence to a lifeline standard…was overly conservative and added to the difficulty and complexity in designing a bridge to meet this standard.[23]

The third study was prepared by Brian Maroney, an engineer with Caltrans and an adjunct professor at the University of California–Davis. Maroney later would be appointed chief engineer for the East Span replacement project and became the principal Caltrans spokesperson whenever the project made news, which was often in the later years of construction. He pursued a lifecycle cost estimate to compare the proposed retrofit and replacement costs. Maroney's estimate for initial construction was $1.167 billion for the viaduct project (higher, but not substantially higher, than the Ventry estimate) and $0.9 billion for the retrofit (slightly higher than the Ventry estimate). Factoring in lifecycle costs, however, raised the retrofit estimate to almost exactly $1 billion, whereas the viaduct option dropped a bit to $1.114 billion. Based on these figures, Maroney recommended just enough retrofit work to ensure safety for the near term while construction of a new viaduct type bridge went forward.[24]

Shortly after Maroney's report was prepared, Caltrans officials adopted the replacement option as departmental policy and began the process of getting the endorsement of Governor Pete Wilson. The biggest hurdle in that effort appears to have been Dean Dunphy, the secretary of Business, Transportation, and Housing, the agency to which Caltrans reported. According to various sources, Dunphy viewed the replacement option with a good deal of skepticism.

The *Oakland Tribune*, presumably working on direct knowledge, reported that Dunphy favored the retrofit option and was furious that the Ventry and SAB reports had been made public in such a coordinated manner, without going through ordinary approval chains.[25] At that time, the *Tribune* and powerful state senator Bill Lockyer were also both in support of retrofit. Lockyer is quoted in an *Oakland Tribune* editorial as saying, "I'm not sure that rebuilding would necessarily make the bridge safer than retrofitting."[26]

After the release of the Ventry and SAB documents and the subsequent release of the Maroney report, the support within the Bay Area for replacement shifted dramatically and Dunphy went along. He signaled his support for the replacement option in a January 10, 1997, memorandum to Governor Wilson. Dunphy cited the estimates from the Maroney report and noted that the replacement option had also been adopted by the two panels established to oversee the seismic retrofit program. Dunphy was referring to the endorsement of the replacement option by the SAB, which had been in existence since 1990, and the peer review panel for the Toll Bridge Retrofit Program, which issued their positions in a joint letter to the director of Caltrans in December 1996. Overall, he observed, "The potential benefits of the new structure far outweigh the risk associated with the additional two years a new bridge will take to complete."[27]

In February 1997, Governor Pete Wilson formally endorsed Dunphy's recommendation but added language that would burden the popular discourse about the Bay Bridge for more than a decade. The governor essentially stated that there were two questions to be answered. The first was replacement versus retrofit; the Wilson administration came out in favor of replacement. The second question had to do with two designs for the replacement structure: the basic viaduct design or a viaduct with some enhanced feature (cable-stayed or SAS) at the shipping channel; Wilson mentioned the cable-stayed structure, which Caltrans favored.

Governor Wilson stated that the viaduct option would cost $1.5 billion, which was $400 million more than Dunphy had suggested only a month earlier. The governor offered no explanation for this huge difference. Wilson stated that the state of California was prepared to build that basic structure. If, however, the "residents of the Bay Area desire an aesthetically enhanced bridge, the additional costs should be borne by the Bay Area."[28] The additional cost for the cable-stayed shipping channel span was thought to be about $200 million.

An aide to Governor Wilson no doubt inflamed Bay Area resentment when he compared building the Bay Bridge to buying a station wagon. The unnamed aide was quoted in various newspaper accounts as saying, "It's like buying a Ford Taurus and getting cloth seats and an AM/FM radio. If you want the leather seats or digital surround sound CD player, you have to pay extra. If the Bay Area wants to pony up the money [for a signature span], they can have it."[29]

There followed two years of wrangling between and among Bay Area leaders and the Wilson administration and later the administration of Governor Gray Davis, between Northern California leaders and Southern California leaders, among differing groups of engineers and other design experts, and an impossibly complex set of other players. By asking the Bay Area to bear the cost of an aesthetically pleasing bridge, Governor Wilson perhaps inadvertently turned over ownership of the bridge design from Caltrans to the political and social leadership of the Bay Area. The agonizing inability of the Bay Area leaders to make a decision about the bridge design and financing is less an indictment of the people of the Bay Area than it is an indictment of the decision-making process. In retrospect, the East Span saga reveals nothing more clearly than that bridge design should not be a democratically arrived-at decision; it is simply too complex for the people and their elected officials to decide.

The other important conclusion about the decision for replacement was that it was based on unsatisfactory cost estimates for both the replacement and retrofit options. It can be said conclusively that the estimate for the replacement option was something like 15 percent of what proved to be the actual cost. It can be said as well that the retrofit estimate was more than five times what had been estimated by Professor Astaneh-Asl only a few years previously. The Wilson administration accepted that recommendation but on the basis of unsatisfactory cost estimates. At that time there was no reason to believe that Caltrans had, through incompetence or deception, offered flawed cost estimates. It did not take long, however, for the entire political hierarchy in the Bay Area and California generally to distrust all figures put forth by Caltrans and to regard the agency with a certain degree of contempt, as did the *San Mateo Times*, when it called Caltrans the "Keystone Kops of construction estimating."[30]

As discussed in the final chapter of this book, the megaproject literature has identified the initial cost estimate as the weakest link in the decision-making process for adopting a costly and potentially disastrous project. The technical experts—in this case, Caltrans and its consultants—controlled the cost estimation process and convinced political leaders to adopt a strategy they might have avoided, had they been given more accurate information.

This miscalculation of project costs is also an area in which the planners of the 1936 and 2013 bridges differed dramatically. Circumstances were such that the 1936 bridge designers were given an upper limit, based on the amount of money the Reconstruction Finance Corporation was prepared to finance. The Bay Bridge designers—the Bay Bridge Division and the consulting engineers—accepted that upper limit, came up with cost estimates that were consistent with it, and made adjustments as necessary to build a bridge within limitations. Political leaders admired them greatly because they had to accept on faith that the cost estimates were legitimate, or as close to accurate as was humanly possible. Had Purcell and Modjeski been off by a factor of five to ten, however, their places in history would be far less exalted than they are today. On the other hand, the 1996 cost estimates prepared by Caltrans were the first step leading to the kind of ridicule printed by the *San Mateo Times* and others. Much of the controversy associated with the 2013 bridge began with the cost estimates made in 1996.

Notes

1. NIST, Special Publication 778, "Performance of Structures during the Loma Prieta Earthquake of October 17, 1989," January 1990. See especially chap. 5, "Performance of Bridge and Highway Structures," by William C. Stone, James D. Cooper, and Nicholas J. Carrino.

2. Ibid., chapter 5, p. 61.

3. George W. Housner and Charles C. Thiel, "Competing Against Time: Report of the Governor's Board of Inquiry on the 1989 Loma Prieta Earthquake," *Earthquake Spectra* 6, no. 4 (2009): 681–711, doi: http://dx.doi.org/10.11931.1585592.

4. Ibid., 56–58. The study notes that significant seismic stabilization work on the East Bay crossing in 1976 had performed well.

5. Through the 1990s the SAB membership was essentially the same as the earlier board of inquiry.

6. In Phase 1 of this program, more than 1,000 single-column bridges were retrofit. Phase 1 retrofit more than 1,100 double-column bridges. The two phases cost about $2.5 billion. "Seismic Retrofit Program," http://www.dot.ca .gov/hq/paffairs/about/retrofit.htm copyright 2016.

7. Abolhassan Astaneh-Asl, "First Draft of Seismic Retrofit Concepts for the Bay Bridge," 1992; Caltrans, "Seismic Retrofit of the San Francisco–Oakland Bay Bridge: Report to the California Transportation Commission," September 10, 1992. As seen in later chapters, Professor Astaneh-Asl would become one of the most outspoken critics of the replacement structure, maintaining that the 1936 bridge was safer than the one that replaced it.

8. http://www.dot.ca.gov/dist4/eastspans/fall97.html

9. Ibid.

10. Caltrans, *San Francisco–Oakland Bay Bridge Seismic Safety Project, Replacement vs. Retrofit*, April 2000.

11. James van Loben Sels to state senators Alfred Alquist, Quentin Kopp, and Larry Bowler, January 13, 1996.

12. As discussed in later chapters, Maroney would emerge as the key figure in the design, management, and construction of the replacement bridge.

13. Caltrans, *Cost Estimate Investigation for a Replacement Structure for the East Spans of the San Francisco–Oakland Bay Bridge* (Sacramento, CA: Office of Structure Design, Caltrans), September 1996.

14. Caltrans, *Cost Estimate Investigation*, 1.

15. Federal Highway Administration, "Value Engineering Final Rule," Federal Highway Administration, U.S. Department of Transportation, Washington, DC, September 5, 2014, https://www.fhwa.dot.gov/ve/

16. Ventry Engineering, The National Constructor's Group, Tokola Corporation, and OPAC Consulting Engineers, *San Francisco–Oakland Bay Bridge, East Bay Crossing Replacement Value Analysis Findings*, Sacramento, CA, December 1996.

17. Frick, "The Making and Un-Making of the San Francisco–Oakland Bay Bridge," 44.

18. "Pursue a New Bridge," *Contra Costa Times*, January 17, 1997.

19. "New Span a Safer Option, Experts Contend," *Oakland Tribune*, January 14, 1997.

20. Caltrans, *Replacement vs. Retrofit*, 5-2.

21. The local press would make quite a point of mocking the fact that the 1936 pilings were timber, even though there is little reason to believe high-quality timber piling not exposed to wet and dry conditions will not last just as well as concrete pilings.

22. "Caltrans May Replace Large Portion of Bay Bridge," *Oakland Tribune*, February 1, 1996.

23. Karen Frick, *Remaking the San Francisco–Oakland Bay Bridge: A Case of Shadowboxing with Nature* (London UK: Routledge, 2015), 159 and associated footnote.

24. Brian Maroney, Caltrans, *Replacement Study for the East Spans of the San Francisco–Oakland Bay Bridge Seismic Safety Project*, December 17, 1996.

25. "Caltrans' Own Scientific Panels Endorse New Bridge over Bay," *Oakland Tribune*, January 9, 1997.

26. Ibid.

27. Dean Dunphy, "Memorandum to Governor Pete Wilson: Consideration of Replacement of the Eastern Spans of the San Francisco–Oakland Bay Bridge," Sacramento, CA, January 10, 1997.

28. Governor Pete Wilson press release, "Wilson Issues Statement After Accepting the Recommendation to Replace the Eastern Spans of the San Francisco–Oakland Bay Bridge: Cites Safety as the Reason to Replace the Eastern Span," Sacramento, CA, February 13, 1997.

29. "Wilson Approves New Bridge but Will Only Pay for Viaduct," *San Francisco Chronicle*, February 13, 1997.

30. "$3 Toll Now Inevitable," *San Mateo Times*, June 17, 2001.

CHAPTER 9

The Context of Great Bridges

Part 2

The world of bridge building changed a great deal in the sixty years between completion of the Bay Bridge in 1936 and the intense discussions of the design of the replacement East Span in 1997 and later. The debate between a reinforced concrete viaduct, a cable-stayed bridge, and an SAS span would not have been possible in 1936 because there were no cable-stayed bridges or SAS spans of the type built in 1936, and the technology for a concrete viaduct with long spans did not exist at that time. In many ways, the debate about the design for the new East Bay span was an attempt by Bay Area residents and political leaders to choose among highly technical and newly developed technologies, some of which they did not understand well. To establish a context for these decisions, it might be useful to summarize the development of the three technologies that were in play in 1997: post-tensioned concrete viaducts, cable-stayed spans, and SAS spans. Each of these technologies were in the experimental stage at the time the 1936 bridge was built, but all three bridge types and forms came into widespread use throughout Europe in the immediate post–World War II era, as that war-torn continent began to rebuild its transportation infrastructure.

Post-Tensioned Concrete Viaducts

Prestressed and post-tensioned concrete technologies are quite similar. In both cases, the rebar in the concrete beam or slab is put under tension by tightening bolts attached to the rebar. With prestressed beams, the rebar is tensioned prior to pouring the concrete. In post-tensioned beams, the rebars are embedded in the concrete and later put under tension by tightening the attached bolts.

The prestressed/post-tensioned system is generally attributed to the great French engineer Eugène Freyssinet, who in 1928 developed a process for prestressing a concrete beam. The technology took off after 1945 in Europe when a shortage of steel caused bridge builders, forced to replace thousands of bridges great and small, to experiment with the prestressing methodology.[1] The technology is more closely aligned with Europe and Asia than with the United States, although it has wide applications in the United States, with both buildings and bridges.

Post-tensioned technologies allow engineers to design bridges of concrete with spans that far exceed what was thought possible in 1936. Caltrans could contemplate an all-viaduct option for the East Span only because this technology made it possible to create concrete spans long enough to accommodate the shipping channel to Oakland Harbor. The proposed spans near Yerba Buena Island were to have reached to 525 feet, a horizontal distance unthinkable with the concrete bridges of the 1930s.

Post-tensioned elements of the Bay Bridge Skyway were precast, post-tensioned, and then hoisted into place, an efficient and relatively risk free means of construction.

Cable-Stayed Spans

Like prestressed concrete bridges, the cable-stayed technology came into widespread use in Europe after World War II. Cable-stayed is generally considered a variant of the suspension bridge, where the cables radiate from a tower rather than being suspended vertically from a larger cable. The earliest such bridges were built in Europe in the mid-1950s. The first cable-stayed highway bridge in the United States was the Sitka Harbor Bridge in Alaska, built in 1972.[2] The best-known cable-stayed bridge in California is the Sundial Bridge, a pedestrian bridge across the Sacramento River in Redding, designed by Santiago Calatrava in 2004. Perhaps the most recognizable cable-stayed bridge in the United States is the Cooper River Bridge in Charleston, South Carolina, completed in 2005. As shown in the Cooper River and Sundial Bridges, the bridge type is amenable to highly architectural treatment and has been used in numerous stunning bridges, chiefly in Europe and Asia.

Santiago Calatrava's Sundial Bridge, Redding. Courtesy of John B. Lovelace Collection of California Photographs in Carol M. Highsmith's America Project in the Carol M. Highsmith Archive.

Self-Anchored Suspension Bridge

The self-anchored suspension bridge, or SAS, is both older and younger than the cable-stayed bridge. An SAS bridge differs from a conventional suspension bridge in that it does not have external anchorages. The West Spans of the Bay Bridge, for example, are anchored in rock in San Francisco and on the west side of Yerba Buena Island. An SAS has no external anchorage. Rather, it relies on the deck to carry the tensile forces that would ordinarily be carried by the external anchorage. Some variations on the SAS date to the late 1850s, when Austrian engineer Josef Langer proposed (but did not build) a suspension bridge anchored in a very thick trussed deck. A bridge built on Langer's principles was constructed in 1870. Several similar bridges were constructed in Germany in the 1910s and 1920s. The earliest SAS bridges in the United States, all still in use, were the Three Sisters, nearly identical bridges across the Allegheny River in Pittsburgh, built in the mid-1920s.[3] As noted in an earlier chapter, the Bay Bridge Division considered using an SAS span for the shipping channel on the 1936 East Bay crossing, where the cantilever span was ultimately built. Had that been built, it would likely have resembled one of the Three Sisters, which were completed only a few years before the Bay Bridge.

Thus, there were working models for the SAS well before there was a usable cable-stayed structure. The cable-stayed technology was widely adopted after 1945 and built in great numbers especially in Europe and Asia. The SAS, however, was rarely adopted and has been used only in special circumstances. David van Goolen, in surveying trends in SAS construction worldwide, concludes, "Although in some cases there was a desire for preventing external anchorages due to the soil conditions, the main reason for choosing the SAS bridge was and still is for aesthetical reasons. The parabolic shaped main cable is still an attractive appearance. It has the same appearance as a conventional suspension bridge." Elsewhere, he notes, "The self-anchored suspension bridge is rarely the cheapest form of bridge design, that is mainly caused by its erection difficulties compared to other bridge types."[4]

Seventh Street Bridge, Pittsburgh. Courtesy of Historic American Engineering Record Collection, Library of Congress.

Engineer van Goolen attributes the rarity of the SAS to the increasing popularity of the cable-stayed bridge. "Before 1955 the German engineers chose to build 4 self-anchored suspension bridges, but after the development of the cable-stayed bridge, the suspension type became an obsolete alternative for a long period of time in Germany and elsewhere. After a period of more than 30 years, a self-anchored suspension bridge was built again (Konohana Bridge, 1990) and was mainly chosen for its aesthetical appearance and the desire for preventing an external anchorage."[5]

Choosing Among Postwar Bridge Technologies

Thus, as the leaders of the Bay Area contemplated the bridge type they preferred for the new East Span, they were asked to choose from among three bridge technologies that effectively were developed in Europe after the end of World War II. Of the three, the prestressed/post-tension concrete bridge had already been used in thousands of bridges in the United States by the time this choice was to be made. The cable-stayed bridge had been built in huge numbers overseas, sparingly in the United States, and never in California, at least for vehicular use. The SAS had rarely been built in the United States or anywhere else in the world during the period 1955 to 1990, when the cable-stayed bridge gained maximum popularity. As van Goolen has noted, the form was revived with the construction of the lovely Konohana Bridge in Osaka, Japan, in 1990. It appears that only two notable SAS bridges were constructed between the Konohana Bridge and the East Span of the Bay Bridge: one in China and one in Belgium.

Unfortunately, the process for selecting a bridge type for the East Span spun out of control in the late 1990s. Caltrans made clear its preference for a viaduct option that relied on the prestressed and/or post-tensioned technologies with which it was familiar and for which it had the required design expertise and cost estimating ability. Local interests, however, particularly those in the East Bay, derisively referred to the Caltrans proposal as a "freeway on stilts," and looked for a more impressive looking structure. The term *signature span* was commonly used to describe the desired alternatives to a viaduct. Beyond the viaduct, the choice essentially lay between a cable-stayed and an SAS signature span. Of these, the cable-stayed option was more reliable in the sense that it could draw from a larger wealth of experience in designing and cost estimating. The ultimate choice, however, was for the SAS, the most daring and least understood of all the available options. That decision drew Caltrans and Bay Area leaders into areas that were fraught with risks for cost overruns, design mistakes, and construction delays, all of which in fact transpired in the troubled years between 1997 and the completion of the bridge in 2013.

Notes

1. A recent analysis of trends in prestressed concrete design is David P. Billington, "Historical Perspective on Prestressed Concrete," *PCI Journal* (January–February 2004): 14–30. Freyssinet's career is analyzed in David P. Billington, *The Tower and the Bridge: The New Art of Structural Engineering* (Princeton, NJ: Princeton University Press, 1985).

2. David P. Billington and Aly Nazmy, "History and Aesthetics of Cable-stayed Bridges," *Journal of Structural Engineering* (1993), vol. 117, no. 10, 352–53.

3. David van Goolen, "Self-Anchored Suspension Bridges," master of science thesis, Delft University of Technology, Delft, Netherlands, 2004. Additional historical information on early SAS bridges is provided in Historic American Engineering Record Collection documentation for the Three Sisters.

4. van Goolen, "Self-Anchored Suspension Bridges," 22.

5. Ibid., 24.

CHAPTER 10

Designing a Megaproject in Public

Governor Wilson's February 1997 announcement, approving a new bridge but leaving its design to the Bay Area, created a situation best described as confused. The executive director of the Metropolitan Transportation Commission (MTC) commented, "Until today, I don't think anybody thought about what the next step would be after Caltrans made the announcement. So everybody's scurrying around trying to figure out what's next."[1] The governor's message suggested there was a simple choice to be made between the viaduct plan, which the state would pay for, and the more expensive cable-stayed option, for which the Bay Area residents would need to make up the difference. By tossing the matter to the local level, however, the governor opened the possibility that additional choices might come forward. Indeed, dozens of different ideas emerged, with no obvious mechanism available to choose from among them.

At the time of the governor's announcement, the Wilson administration had already decided to turn to the MTC to decide which way to go: with the viaduct or with some type of signature span. This was a peculiar decision in that it went far beyond the type of decision for which the MTC was created. The MTC is a regional transportation planning agency under California state law and a metropolitan planning organization under federal law.[2] In both instances, the MTC is the designated body of coordinating transportation projects and for making key decisions for allocating state and federal transportation funds. It emphatically is not a body intended to decide the appropriate bridge type for a particular crossing. But that was the assignment given to the MTC by the Wilson administration, a decision that led to many years of frustration and controversy.

The Bay Bridge Design Task Force Meets

Shortly after the Wilson administration assigned it design respon-
sibilities for the East Span replacement, MTC leadership established a single-purpose committee, called the Bay Bridge Design
Task Force. While the MTC as a whole represents nine counties,
the task force had members drawn from only four of those counties: San Francisco, Alameda, Contra Costa, and Solano. The task
force also included a representative from the Bay Conservation
and Development Commission, a state-created agency with re-
sponsibilities for managing Bay resources. Chaired by Alameda
County supervisor Mary King, the nine-member task force included Oakland mayor Elihu Harris, Contra Costa County supervisor Mark DeSaulnier, and San Pablo city council member Sharon
Price. Also on board were Jon Rubin, appointed by the mayor of
San Francisco, San Francisco supervisor Tom Hsish, Suisun City
mayor Jim Spering, and Angela Siracusa from the Bay Conservation and Development Commission.[3]

The Bay Bridge Design Task Force in turn appointed the Engineering and Design Advisory Panel (EDAP), comprising engineers and architects. The EDAP membership changed over time
but generally comprised thirty-five members, with an engineer
from URS Corporation as its chair and an architect from Skid-
more, Owings, and Merrill as its vice-chair.[4] The MTC at this
point had nearly fifty people advising it on the bridge design. Caltrans brought the number even higher by creating its own panel
to work parallel to the EDAP. This group, the Caltrans Advisory
Panel on Conceptual Designs, was charged with passing technical
judgment on any plan brought forth by the EDAP. The advisory
panel included some public servants from Caltrans and some professionals from structural engineering firms; the chair was Charles
Seim, an engineer with T. Y. Lin International.[5]

These various committees and task forces met dozens of times
between March 1997 and June 1998, usually in well-attended
public meetings. The EDAP, for example, met twenty-three times
between March 1997 and June 1998.[6] This panel in particular
wrestled with how best to make the new bridge conform to its

own setting east of Yerba Buena Island and to the larger setting that included the suspension spans west of the island. As a first matter, the EDAP in April 1997 adopted as a guiding principle the harmonizing of the new span with both its natural and its structural settings. The principle, however, was so nuanced as to accommodate just about any idea presented to the panel: "The bridge should integrate into the site and the surrounding environment by reflecting the grand scale of the San Francisco Bay, by harmonizing with the existing west span of the bridge by landing gracefully on the Oakland and Yerba Buena landfalls. The replacement bridge by contrast or similarity, [should] complement the existing San Francisco bridge suspension span. They should feel related in some way that makes the two bridge elements into a whole. One bridge should not diminish the visual quality or importance of the other."[7]

In May 1997 the EDAP committee conducted a three-day public workshop on the design of the new bridge. While committee members and Caltrans hoped to discuss only the signature span near Yerba Buena Island, they received suggestions for widely and often wildly different concepts for the entire structure.[8]

The serious business of the workshop, however, focused on the three fundamental approaches to crossing: continuation of the viaduct, several variations of a cable-stayed main span, and the SAS span. Following the three-day workshop the EDAP was unable to decide between the SAS and the cable-stayed options, and requested Caltrans to carry to 30 percent design the two alternatives, arguing that more information was needed on cost and design feasibility before an informed decision could be made.[9] Caltrans rejected this request, stating, "Caltrans is of the opinion that information exists to clearly differentiate among the various choices associated with the new Bay Bridge."[10]

Ultimately, Caltrans relented and awarded a contract to carry both designs to 30 percent, hiring a joint venture of T. Y. Lin and Moffatt & Nichol. This contract was awarded in late 1997, leading to many more public hearings but focused on the three possible options: skyway, SAS, and cable-stayed.

The Design Options before the Engineering and Design Advisory Panel

The EDAP was populated chiefly by architects and engineers and it would have the first say on what type of bridge was right for this crossing. The EDAP, however, was not the only group interested in this subject. The larger Bay Bridge Design Task Force was populated chiefly by elected officials who responded to wider interests than the EDAP. With dozens of elected officials and appointees considering what to do with the East Bay crossing, there were, of course, widely divergent points of view. To summarize these many perspectives, it is useful to focus on three major issues that were discussed: the total aesthetics of the bridge, the aesthetics of SAS versus cable-stayed, and the buildability and safety of the options.

Total Aesthetics of the Bridge

During the pivotal year of discussions by the EDAP, only three options truly received serious consideration: building a skyway, building a skyway with a cable-stayed main span, or building a skyway with an SAS main span. The fourth option—retrofitting the 1936 bridge—was already rejected by state officials before the EDAP was created, but that option found its way back into all discussions about the East Bay crossing.

Of these four, only two had what might be considered a unified design, one with a consistent design for the entire structure from the Oakland touchdown to the Yerba Buena tunnel. The 1936 bridge had a unified design, even though it used three basic bridge types. All three types were muscular metal trusses with a consistent pattern of diagonals and verticals across the entire length. Retrofitting the 1936 bridge would have given a consistent design. The other design with a total aesthetic spanning the entire length was the skyway, which had a unified appearance from one end to the other.

The retrofit option was effectively abandoned in 1997 and was only rarely considered after that point. Occasionally, San Francisco mayor Willie Brown, frustrated with negotiating with Caltrans and other Bay Area leaders, would recommend the process go back to retrofit. In April 1999, for example, Mayor Brown, dissatisfied with the work of the EDAP and the MTC, wrote to state senator Tom Torlakson, recommending that the state abandon the replacement project and go back to a retrofit option.[11] Brown's support for retrofit, however, was based on safety concerns about the replacement alternative, not on the aesthetics of the 1936 bridge.

The skyway option had a few supporters, chiefly on the basis of its unified appearance. Alan Hess is an architect, architectural historian, and architectural critic for the *San Jose Mercury News*. In an article entitled "A Bridge to Take Us from Whimsy to Expensive Looniness," he wrote, "The fact is that a bold engineering statement simply isn't needed. The skyway proposed last year was a simple thread rising with the least amount of fuss and the most slender profile from the Oakland mudflats to the Yerba Buena tunnel. It would have given the bay the gift of simplicity. It would complement, rather than compete with, its surroundings. With some polish, its rhythmic pylons lifting the roadbed from the waters could have been svelte sculpture—the very best of Caltrans freeway architecture, mating solid practical engineering with breathtaking kinetic sculpture."[12]

A more common statement in favor of unified design was a criticism that even the SAS and cable-stayed options were still fundamentally skyways with a signature span tacked on to them. This opinion was expressed by many, including Terry Roberts, public works director for the city of Oakland:

> Our concern stems from the fact that the two "signature" design options under consideration are 85 percent viaduct. As proposed, the distinguishing architectural features of these two options would be located adjacent to Yerba Buena Island and constitute only 15 percent of the overall bridge length. Unfortunately, the rest of the bridge resembles an undistinguished freeway overpass. The existing bridge span has more architectural design features than either of the proposed signature structures. I hope you concur that we in Oakland and the East Bay deserve a more befitting gateway to our front door. The next step in the design process must evaluate what architectural design

improvements can be made to the viaduct portion of the new bridge.[13]

There was also a brief outpouring of support for reviving Frank Lloyd Wright's Butterfly design (see chapter 7), which he had developed for the southern crossing, which was in a different setting with different foundation considerations. Those who supported the Butterfly design did so on the basis of the integrated design.

In the end, there was too little support for the retrofit, skyway, or Butterfly design options. The principal debate, then, was concentrated on whether the SAS or the cable-stayed signature span would win acceptance.

Aesthetics of SAS vs. Cable-Stayed

As noted, in late 1997 Caltrans issued a contract to the consortium of T. Y. Lin International and Moffatt & Nichol to develop 30 percent designs for the two leading signature span contenders. Between March and July 1997 the EDAP had eliminated all alternatives other than the SAS and cable-stayed options. This winnowing out allowed them to seek expensive design work for a limited number of choices.

The T. Y. Lin–Moffatt & Nichol consortium, in turn, hired two outside groups to lead the design, one for each option. It hired MacDonald Architects of San Francisco to design the SAS, assisted by senior engineer Herbert Rothman of Weidlinger Associates. The work on the cable-stayed option was led by H2L2 Architects/ Planners, an East Coast architectural firm. The two firms and the Weidlinger engineers had considerable work experience on high-profile bridges. H2L2's website lists a number of important bridges that it helped design, including three notable cable-stayed structures: the Cooper River Bridge in Charleston, South Carolina; the New Mississippi River Bridge in St. Louis; and the Quinnipiac Bridge in New Haven.[14] MacDonald Architects' website claims design responsibility for dozens of bridges, most in California and most of standard concrete girder design. The firm also claims architectural responsibility for the big Ohio River Bridge in Louisville, which is a cable-stayed structure. Interestingly, MacDonald, like H2L2, claims design responsibility for the big Cooper River

Bridge, one of the best-known cable-stayed bridges in the country. In his book *Bay Bridge*, Donald MacDonald is straightforward in claiming to have designed the Cooper River Bridge. Speaking of himself in third person, he writes, "Heading one subgroup, the one that eventually came up with the self-anchored suspension bridge, was the San Francisco architect Donald MacDonald, designer of the country's longest cable-stayed bridge (Cooper River in Charleston, SC)."[15] The websites of the two firms also both claim design of the East Bay 2013 SAS, as does Weidlinger on its website: "Weidlinger Associates designed the world's longest self-anchored suspension bridge, with a main span of 385 meters."[16] In a recent profile on Herbert Rothman in *Progressive Engineer*, Rothman is credited with designing the SAS:

> Recently, a new one [bridge] has emerged as his pet: the San Francisco Oakland Bay Bridge. The mammoth crossover actually consists of two tandem suspension bridges, a tunnel that comes out on an island, then a long cantilevered bridge, and finally a long viaduct to Oakland. Rothman was chief engineer for a project to replace the east span, the cantilevered section. "The long cantilever wouldn't stand up under a big earthquake, and Caltrans decided it would make more sense to start over than reinforce it," he explains. For resisting seismic activity, he came up with an SAS bridge, meaning the ends of the cables are connected to the bridge deck, rather than anchored in massive concrete on land. It ranks as the world's longest SAS bridge.[17]

To note these multiple claims for design responsibility does not call into question the veracity of any of the three firms; doubtless both MacDonald and H2L2 participated in the Cooper River Bridge and all three are known to have participated in the design of the 2013 Bay Bridge signature span. Rather, it points out the difficulty in assigning to any one person or firm responsibility for the design of structures as complex as the Cooper River Bridge or the 2013 Bay Bridge.

What is notable, however, is that none of the participating firms—MacDonald, H2L2, or Weidlinger—claims any prior experience with SAS design. As noted in chapter 9, no one in the

Lenny Zakim Bridge, Boston. Courtesy of Carol M. Highsmith, Library of Congress.

United States had worked on an SAS, simply because none had been built here since the very different SAS types of the late 1920s.

During much of 1997 and 1998 the two teams worked to develop the most desirable version of a cable-stayed or SAS, appropriate to the specific site near Yerba Buena Island. Donald MacDonald chronicles the design process in sketches and in text. Both teams explored similar variations: one tower with radiating cables, or three towers carrying the two decks with cables set in four groups (two for each deck).

In June 1998 the two teams presented to the EDAP 30 percent designs for the SAS and cable-stayed options. The two were actually similar in appearance in that each proposed a single tall and slender tower with cables to support the roadway. The difference was in the array of the cables. The cable-stayed option relied on thinner cables radiating in progressively longer reaches. Its appearance would have been somewhat similar to the Bunker Hill Bridge, part of the Big Dig in Boston, but without the wishbone shape to the tower and with a single tower instead of the two in Boston.

The SAS proposal called for a four-legged tower, joined to appear as a single unit. The tower supported a saddle with four openings for the cable. The cable has the sway typical of suspension bridges, rather than the rigid appearance of cables in a cable-stayed bridge.

In June 1998 the EDAP made its choice and opted for the SAS. The vote of the panel, held on May 30, 1998, was twelve to seven in favor of the SAS design. We know a little about the basis for this decision because of Donald MacDonald's book. According to MacDonald, the choice came not in a single meeting but a series of meetings with the EDAP and the SAS and cable-stayed teams. He writes, "Detailed arguments pro and con ensued, with numerous and lengthy meetings before the Design Advisory Panel. The process began in November 1997 and ended in June 1998 with the unexpected selection of the self-anchored suspension bridge, designed by MacDonald and Rothman. The vote of the panel, held on May 30, 1998, was twelve to seven recommending the self-anchored form to the Metropolitan Transportation Commission, which endorsed the recommendation."[18]

Both the SAS and the cable-stayed designs were being explored because the Bay Area leaders were unhappy with the aesthetics of the skyway design. Not surprisingly, the decision for the SAS over cable-stayed was based chiefly on aesthetic considerations. MacDonald explains how he successfully pitched the SAS to the panel, again referring to himself in third person: "MacDonald successfully argued for the self-anchored suspension span partly because the Bay Area had a strong tradition of suspension bridges and the design would complete the necklace of suspension structures around the region. With its distinctive single tower 525 feet high, its convex shape opposite the concave form of the main cables, relates the silhouette of the bridge to the shape of the East Bay hills beyond."[19]

This winning argument was quite unlike the language the designers of the 1936 bridge used to defend their choices of bridge types. As shown in chapter 5 aesthetics were a major consideration in 1936 but the language used at that time was far different from that in 1998. It is difficult to imagine Purcell or Modjeski referring to completion of a necklace of bridges or the opposing concave swoop of the West Span suspension structure and the convex form of, say, Telegraph Hill.

Even though EDAP made the decision on aesthetic grounds, it did not satisfy the tastes of all East Bay leaders. Oakland mayor Jerry Brown opined in the *San Francisco Chronicle* on June 22, "The recommended design—half a suspension bridge attached to a bland viaduct—speaks of mediocrity, not greatness.... It mocks the principle of the suspension bridge by eradicating its most beautiful part: the freely suspended towers.... It fails to rise to the challenge which the setting and new millennium demand. It could be anywhere."[20]

Mayor Brown's objection came too late in the process and MTC ignored it, and approved the SAS design in late June.

Buildability and Safety of the Options

The selection of the SAS was made by a majority of voting members of the EDAP, some of whom were engineers, some architects, and some neither. It is clear from the foregoing that the decision hinged principally on aesthetics.

The greatest criticism of the decision came from bridge engineers—not on aesthetics, but on the basis of buildability and safety.[21] Two giants of the structural engineering field in California—T. Y. Lin and Abolhassan Astaneh-Asl—treated the decision as a disaster. A member of the EDAP, T. Y. Lin, voted against the SAS design. The vote reflected "an ignorance in engineering." He warned that the decision "will be a testament to our ignorance. We'll be the laughingstock of the whole world."[22]

Professor Astaneh-Asl was equally sharp in his criticism. His critique focused on two unknowns: whether a SAS could be made seismically safe, and whether it could be built without major construction problems. In June 1998 he wrote to the MTC, stating, "I am convinced that if the proposed self-anchored bridge is constructed and the Hayward fault ruptures, there is a high probability that the resulting earthquake can severely damage this bridge and cause partial or catastrophic failure of the main span (during construction and/or after completion)." He also pointed to the fact that almost no SAS bridges had been built in recent decades and worried that the lack of experience could lead to design, fabrication, and construction problems.[23]

Lin and Astaneh-Asl continued to criticize the design, especially after many of the buildability and safety issues they predicted came to pass in the coming years. Another concern, one closely associated with the buildability issue, was the cost of the SAS span. Beginning in 2001 Caltrans began to revise upward its cost estimate for the entire East Span replacement project. Whenever possible, Caltrans attempted to pin the responsibility for overruns on the MTC because it had taken so long to make a decision and because it had decided on the SAS signature span. While it is likely the SAS decision contributed greatly to increased costs, it is also extremely unlikely that the SAS caused costs to go up by a factor of five or six.

The SAS Design Is Finally Approved, 1998–2001

By July 1998 the MTC had done half what Governor Wilson had asked of it. Wilson's charge to the MTC was to decide on a bridge type and, if something other than the skyway, to figure out how to pay for it. In deciding on the SAS, the MTC fulfilled half of its obligation. It took some time, however, to solve the funding riddle.

The momentum gained by the MTC decision spurred equally decisive action by Caltrans. The SAS decision gave Caltrans a preferred alternative to analyze in its "Environmental Impact Statement for the East Bay Replacement."[24] In November 1998 Caltrans and the Federal Highway Administration certified the adequacy of the impact statement.[25] That momentum faltered, however, and for several years Caltrans wrestled with two unrelated but equally troublesome developments: a feud with the U.S. Navy over access to Yerba Buena Island, and emerging difficulties with the California legislature over the projected costs of the project.

The feud with the Navy was also in part a quarrel with the city and county of San Francisco, which intended to take over Yerba Buena and Treasure Islands when the Navy left the area. In addition to selecting a bridge type, the MTC was responsible for determining an alignment for the bridge, either north or south of the

1936 span. San Francisco favored the southern alignment because it inflicted less damage to historic U.S. Navy buildings on Yerba Buena Island dating back to the early twentieth century.[26] The Port of Oakland and the Coast Guard favored the northern alignment because it caused less disruption to the operations of both the port and the active Coast Guard facility on Yerba Buena. This issue was secondary to most problems with the replacement project but certainly could not be ignored because construction could not begin until the Navy transferred the land necessary to build the island touchdown and make necessary modifications to on- and off-ramps. The impasse was ultimately resolved in May 2000, when the Navy transferred the necessary land to the U.S. Department of Transportation, which transferred it to Caltrans, bypassing the entire Base Realignment and Closure process.[27]

A more ominous threat to the project came in early 2001, when Caltrans released an update to its cost estimates. The original estimates of about $1 billion in 1996 had already been raised to $2.6 billion in 1997. The 2001 estimate ballooned this figure to $4.6 billion.[28] The implications of this and later cost estimate increases will be discussed in greater detail in chapter 11. For present purposes, the new increase, nearly doubling the previous estimate and quadrupling the original number, made it extremely difficult for Bay Area leaders to make good on their commitment to pay for the signature span. True, the SAS had almost certainly contributed to this increase but it could not be blamed entirely for such drastic inflation.

Bay Area leaders were furious. Senator Don Perata initially recommended that Caltrans return to the retrofit option. Subsequently, however, Perata announced, "I don't think anyone is interested in going back to the beginning. I don't want to reopen the debate on the retrofit."[29]

Following much hand-wringing, the legislature devised a compromise, wrapped up in Assembly Bill 1171, introduced by assembly member John Dutra. Dutra's legislation wrote into state law all meaningful aspects of the replacement bridge. It would be built on the northern alignment and would feature a single-tower SAS main span. The Legislature also sealed in place a formula by which the already inflated costs and any future cost overruns would be handled, with costs roughly divided between toll increases and increased payments of state and federal funds.

With that, the messy business of designing the bridge was finished. Meanwhile, the even messier task of building the bridge was just getting under way.

Notes

1. Erin McCormick, "Cost vs. Aesthetics: Bridging the Gap," *San Francisco Examiner*, February 14, 1997.

2. The MTC's website includes a detailed discussion of its obligations under federal transportation law and under various aspects of state law.

3. Frick, "The Making and Un-Making of the San Francisco–Oakland Bay Bridge," 43.

4. Ibid., 44.

5. Ibid.

6. MTC, "East Bay Span Replacement."

7. Frick, "The Making and Un-Making of the San Francisco–Oakland Bay Bridge," 46.

8. Among the rejected proposals was the call for tall office buildings in the Bay, with the bridge suspended between them and an old proposal, developed by Frank Lloyd Wright's Taliesin West in the 1940s, for a fanciful concrete viaduct. Wright's design, however, was meant for the much shallower waters of the southern crossing.

9. The term *30 percent design* refers to a stage of design that is more specific than a concept but far less detailed than a construction document. The 30 percent stage is used to test cost assumptions and other major considerations.

10. Frick, "The Making and Un-Making of the San Francisco–Oakland Bay Bridge," 86.

11. Brown to Torlakson, April 5, 1999, included in an appendix to Caltrans, *Replacement vs. Retrofit*.

12. Alan Hess, "A Bridge to Take Us from Whimsy to Expensive Looniness," *San Jose Mercury News* (April 5, 1998).

13. Roberts letter to Mary King, MTC Bay Bridge Design Task Force, July 8, 1997.

14. The H2L2 website is found at www.h2l2/infrastructure. The Quinnipiac is not technically a cable-stayed bridge, but it resembles one.

15. Donald MacDonald and Ira Nadel, *Bay Bridge: History and Design of a New Icon* (San Francisco, CA: Chronicle Books, 2013), 53.

16. "San Francisco Oakland Bay Bridge," Weidlinger Associates (now part of Thornton Tomasetti), http://www.thorntontomasetti.com/

17. "Profiles: Herbert Rothman," *Progressive Engineer*, February 2002. Rothman was in his seventies when he worked on the Bay Bridge

18. MacDonald and Nadel, *Bay Bridge*, 61.

19. Ibid., 61.

20. "Bay Bridge Decision Needs Further Review," *San Francisco Chronicle*, June 22, 1998.

21. We use the term *buildability* to mean the degree to which the engineering profession is capable of designing and building a bridge of a particular type.

22. T. Y. Lin quoted in Frick, "The Making and Un-Making of the San Francisco–Oakland Bay Bridge," 59.

23. Astaneh-Asl quoted in ibid., 62.

24. Caltrans, *Environmental Impact Statement: San Francisco–Oakland Bay Bridge East Spans Seismic Safety Project*. November 1998.

25. MTC, "East Bay Span Replacement."

26. Frick, *Remaking the San Francisco–Oakland Bay Bridge* includes a long chapter on this dispute involving San Francisco, the Navy, and Caltrans. By coincidence, the Navy was completing environmental review for transferring Yerba Buena Island to San Francisco at the same time Caltrans was completing studies for replacing the East Span. The Navy had committed to preserving historic buildings on Yerba Buena Island as part of its Base Realignment and Closure review. Those commitments were threatened by the northern alignment.

27. "East Span's Drama, Delays," *San Francisco Chronicle*, August 24, 2013. This is a major retrospective article on the travails in planning the replacement span.

28. MTC, "East Bay Span Replacement."

29. Perata quoted in Frick, "The Making and Un-Making of the San Francisco–Oakland Bay Bridge," 182.

CHAPTER 11

Everything That Can Go Wrong...

With passage of Assembly Bill 1171 in October 2001, all aspects of the bridge design had literally been written into law: the alignment and the bridge type were mentioned specifically in the law, settling the long debate over those two issues. Nothing remained for Caltrans to do but to build the megaproject, which the agency accomplished twelve years later at a cost of nearly $7 billion.

During the course of those twelve years, Caltrans experienced a frustrating series of setbacks relating to the cost of the structure, the safety of the bridge type, and even the professionalism of the Caltrans personnel involved in construction management. For those most intimately connected to the project, that twelve-year span made up a major part of their careers and was a challenging and sometimes frustrating experience.

The Basic Design of the 2013 Bridge

To appreciate some of the construction challenges the bridge posed, it is useful to summarize the basic design of the structure, particularly the most innovative aspects of it. The skyway or viaduct section of the bridge accounts for about 85 percent of its length. It comprises a series of concrete box girders on concrete piers, which, in turn, rest on tubular steel piles. The signature span is a single-tower SAS span, supporting steel box girder roadways that conform to the concrete girders on the viaduct. The SAS tower is carried on concrete piles. The viaduct and SAS are discussed separately below.

The skyway comprises a series of relatively short (about five hundred feet each) concrete box girder spans, arranged in side-by-side roadway decks, each deck carried on a concrete column, atop a concrete pier on tubular steel pilings. The box girders are built of precast, post-tensioned concrete segments, each twenty-five feet long. Altogether there are 452 of these precast segments, each of which was constructed in Stockton, California, and taken to the site by barge. The most distinctive element of the skyway design was the use of two metal pipes, embedded within each box girder segment. When the segments were joined a flexible buffer, or fuse, was installed between the lengths of the metal pipe; this buffer was made to deform in the event of an earthquake, minimizing damage to the concrete segments.[1]

No major construction problems plagued the skyway. The structure was designed by a partnership of T. Y. Lin International and Moffatt & Nichol, as was the SAS signature span. With the exception of the unusual fuses between the metal pipe sections, the design and construction for the skyway followed methodologies perfected in hundreds if not thousands of concrete box girder structures built in California and elsewhere.

The Self-Anchored Suspension Span

The SAS is an asymmetrical single tower suspension bridge, with a 590-foot span west of the tower (mostly over Yerba Buena Island) and a 1,263-foot span to the east, forming the shipping channel below the bridge.

Consistent with the overall design of any SAS, the cable for the bridge is embedded in the roadway, and not in external anchorages. The cable path is a complex weaving around three piers and a single tower. The cable is attached in anchorage boxes below Pier W-2, which is a land-based pier. The cable rises to the single tower in a roughly 45-degree angle and is linked to a huge saddle atop the 525-foot tower. The cable splays out again to reach the edge of the roadway at the end of the much longer shipping channel span. The cable wraps around the end of the two roadway girders at Pier E-2. The cable then returns to the saddle at the top of the tower and back to the saddles at Pier W-2. The continuous cable measures about one mile.

The tower is an interesting four-legged structure, with four pentagonal metal shafts, joined by horizontal struts. The struts include shear links that will allow the tower to flex in the event of an earthquake.

Nothing about the design of the SAS can be considered typical or routine. Among its peculiarities are the fact that it is a single

tower rather than double towers. The only other major SAS structure built at the turn of the twenty-first century was the Konahana
Bridge in Japan, which used two towers. The Bay Bridge SAS also
had an exceptionally long main span, nearly 40 percent longer
than the Konohana Bridge, which was the longest SAS at the time
it was built in 1990. Because it was erected in a seismically active
zone, the Bay Bridge SAS incorporated a great number of features
designed for seismic safety. It is also unique within the context of
the Bay Bridge in that the structure is all steel, except for the concrete in its piers.

Persistent Cost Overruns and Construction Delays

Assembly Bill 1171 passed in October 2001; in January 2002, Governor Gray Davis officiated at a groundbreaking ceremony held
on Treasure Island within sight of the 1936 East Span. He declared
the new bridge would be opened in five years and called it a "great
undertaking."[2] Shortly before the ceremony, Caltrans began to
open bids for the job, which was broken into a series of contracts.
The largest of the contract bids opened in 2002 was for construction of the viaduct or skyway, which came in at $1.04 billion, one-
third higher than Caltrans had estimated.[3]

The $300 million overrun for the skyway was troubling but
less so than the chronic delays in construction. In early 2002 Caltrans reported to the legislature that the westbound lanes would
open in late 2005 and the eastbound lanes in 2007. In June 2002,
Caltrans revised its estimate for completion, promising that both
directions of traffic would be completed in 2009.[4]

The situation went from bad to worse in early 2003. On January 21 Caltrans released a request for quotation for the first construction elements for the SAS signature span, that being the
marine tower, tower T-1, the key support for the single-tower
design. Several leading bridge construction firms immediately informed Caltrans they would not be bidding because the cost estimate was much too low and the construction schedule unrealistic.
In May Caltrans amended the request for quotation, extending the
deadline for bidding on the marine foundation to August 2003
and all but eliminating the Buy American provision, in the hope
that the use of non-American steel would bring down the cost.

Governor Gray Davis, at January 29, 2002, groundbreaking on Treasure Island. Courtesy of *San Francisco Chronicle*, January 30, 2002; John Blanchard/*San Francisco Chronicle*/Polaris.

The bids were opened on August 19. A single bid came in from the American Bridge Company and it was 63 percent higher than the Caltrans estimate: $210 million versus the estimated $129 million.[5] In October 2003 Caltrans rejected the bid.

The inability to attract a bidder for T-1 is somewhat surprising in that the bidding took place at a time of economic crisis in California and much of the rest of the United States. An economic downturn, often called the dot-com bubble recession, was joined by an energy crisis in the early years of the twenty-first century. The recession and energy crisis greatly depressed revenue available to state government and resulted in huge revenue shortfalls. In August 2003 critics of Governor Davis submitted sufficient signatures to force a recall election, designed to force him from office. On October 7 Davis was recalled (the first such recall in California history) and, in the same election, Arnold Schwarzenegger was elected governor.[6]

Between the October 2003 recall and December of 2004, the overall Bay Bridge replacement project continued forward slowly. The contract for T-1 was not let but work proceeded on construction of the skyway leading to it, as well as on the land-based pier on Yerba Buena Island, called Pier W-2. Bridge construction was proceeding as if the SAS were to be built but nothing directly related to the SAS, other than Pier W-2, was under construction.

On December 10, 2004, the still-young Schwarzenegger administration sent the Bay Bridge replacement project into crisis mode. Governor Schwarzenegger announced that he favored a return to the skyway-only alternative for the East Bay crossing. This decision seemingly sent discussions back to where they were before the passage of Assembly Bill 1171 in late 2001.[7] This chaotic situation brought out critics from the left and right, attacking nearly everyone involved with the process but reserving special venom for Caltrans. Senator Don Perata, a Democrat, observed, "The same agency that botched the last estimate is the same agency recommending we build the skyway, saying it won't take any longer and promising it will save money. I'm not sure there's a lot of confidence in Caltrans there."[8] Senator Tom McClintock, a Republican, said of the East Span project, "It's the biggest fiasco in California transportation history. This was a simple retrofit of that bridge that has been botched beyond anyone's wildest imagination."[9]

Members of the California legislature were forced to choose between sticking with the SAS design, as they had specified years earlier, and going along with the administration's proposal to return to the skyway-only alternative. The nature of the decision was summarized in a January 2005 report of the Legislative Analyst's Office (LAO): "Hard Decisions before the Legislature: Toll Bridge Seismic Retrofit."[10]

The LAO report highlighted one problem in monitoring the costs of the East Span replacement: the fact that its costs were commonly buried in very large appropriations for the entire seismic retrofit program, or as part of an appropriation specific to the toll bridges statewide. By 2005, however, most retrofit work had been accomplished; all that remained was the East Span replacement and a small amount of work on the Richmond–San Rafael

Bridge. The LAO could focus on the East Span project because it alone required a "hard decision." The analysis laid out how costs had ballooned from $1 billion in 1997 to $5.1 billion in 2004. It also made the case that the decision was not between totally different designs, since the skyway had always made up most of the bridge, irrespective of the main span, and much of the skyway was already built in 2005.

The LAO focused the task before the legislature as involving two critical decisions that had to be made and made soon. The first was: Should the Bay Bridge East Span be redesigned? The second was: How shall the program be funded? The LAO concluded that, at such a late date, the savings associated with redesign were minimal and the risks of delay and cost overruns were huge. "Thus, the Legislature faces a choice between an existing Bay Bridge design (SAS) that is known to be expensive and complicated to construct, but that has already completed the difficult design and environmental processes; and a redesign (skyway or cable-stayed) that initially has the potential to save money, but that could end up taking longer and costing more due to risks in the environmental and design phases."[11]

The LAO never overtly recommended that the legislature stick with the costly but known SAS design. Between the lines, however, that seemed to be the LAO's preference. In terms of how this work should be paid for, the LAO laid out a series of unattractive options, most involving increasing the Bay Bridge tolls or redirecting toll funding from other projects.

These "hard decisions" were made by the legislature when it passed Assembly Bill 144, introduced by Assemblyperson Loni Hancock of Berkeley. The bill established the bridge type: the previously approved SAS. And it established a complex formula in which a greater percentage of the costs would be borne by toll-paying users of the bridge, a concession needed to get the support of the Schwarzenegger administration. The legislation also created yet another oversight committee: the Toll Bridge Program Oversight Committee. The committee comprised the major players who had governed the process in the past: (1) the MTC and its Bay Area Toll Authority, (2) Caltrans, and (3) the California Transportation Commission. Among other things, the Toll Bridge

Program Oversight Committee was given final authority for issuing bid documents and for approving any bids.[12]

In August 2005 the committee approved new specifications and bid documents for the SAS. The design was essentially the same. Two major changes were an increase in the estimate to $1.5 billion, double the 2004 estimate; and total elimination of the Buy American requirement.[13] The law also allowed construction to resume on the tower for the SAS. The job had been awarded to Kiewit-FCI-Marston in April 2004 but the work had been suspended when the administration decided to abandon the SAS. (This was a joint venture of Kiewit Corporation, FCI Constructors, and Marston Construction.)

Assembly Bill 144 resolved finally all issues regarding the design and costs for the bridge. In mid-April 2006 the Toll Bridge Program Oversight Committee accepted a bid from American Bridge/Fluor to construct the SAS for $1.43 billion, beating out a $1.68 billion bid by another joint venture headed by Kiewit.[14] This allowed construction to proceed on all remaining elements of the Bay Bridge East Span, including the foundation work for the SAS and the SAS itself. It also all but ensured that the steel fabrication work, the costliest aspect of the SAS job, would be outsourced to China, and set in motion a potential quality-control issue, because neither Caltrans nor American Bridge/Fluor were able to enforce quality standards on the Chinese subcontractors.

Construction Oversight of Concrete Work by Caltrans Goes Awry

In early 2009 a routine audit of overtime abuse at Caltrans blew up into a major controversy, calling into question the structural integrity of Pier T-1. The structural elements involved in this scandal were less important than later construction problems but were significant nevertheless. By 2009 it was clear the bridge was hugely expensive and far behind schedule. The emerging cost overrun scandal initiated a series of investigations that also asked whether the new structure was unsafe.

The California Bureau of State Audits (BSA) is responsible, among its many duties, for managing the Whistleblower Protection Act of 1993, or Whistleblower Act, through which the agency investigates credible claims of improper activities by state employees. In 2009 the agency received an anonymous tip that two Caltrans employees, Duane Wiles and Walter Wyllie, were charging overtime for time not worked. The BSA requested copies of all timesheets for the two employees. In its 2013 report, BSA heavily criticized Caltrans for its slow response to this request and for its general inaction.[15]

Caltrans' tardiness might be explained in part by the fact that it had in early 2009 received even more disturbing reports that Duane Wiles had not only lied about overtime but had falsified test results on bridge foundations, including tests on the foundation at the T-1 pier that was to hold the main tower for the SAS portion of the East Span.

Wiles and Wyllie worked in the Foundation Testing Branch, which is part of the Geotechnical Services office and is responsible for performing tests on bridge piers or other foundations to ensure they can perform as designed. At the time, the branch was supervised by Brian Liebich, a civil engineer with considerable experience in geotechnical work. Wiles and his coworker worked as technicians and were not civil engineers; they were paid on an hourly basis. They were involved in two types of tests: the gamma gamma test and pile load tests. Both were designed to test the integrity of concrete used in foundation work. The gamma gamma test measures density in concrete by emitting radiation at select locations. Pile load testing is more of a mechanical test in which a pile or pier is loaded with heavy beams and physically stressed until it fails. The pile load work earns a technician an additional $1.25 per hour, as negotiated in the collective bargaining agreement for that class.

The whistleblower accused Wiles and Wyllie of two types of fraud. First, this person accused them of claiming overtime work when they did not in fact work overtime. Second, he or she accused them of claiming the pile load differential, when they did not actually perform the tests as claimed. The BSA was principally concerned with this type of timesheet fraud; the auditors were not technically in a position to pass judgment on the larger claim of fraud in the actual test results. By early 2010 the BSA auditors were able to acquire and analyze 2008 timesheets for Wiles and

Wyllie and concluded the two in one year had been awarded at least $13,788 in overpayment, including fraudulent overtime and differential pay claims.[16]

The BSA auditors then turned their attention to Brian Liebich, who had signed all of those fraudulent timesheets. They had two reasons to look into Liebich's performance. First, the overtime fraud by Wiley and his associate was so blatant that it represented negligence on Liebich's part, for not noticing and/or disciplining his employees. Second, BSA had been alerted in yet another whistleblower call that Liebich had used Wiley and Wyllie to carry material and do work on a remote property Liebich owned near Susanville, California, nearly two hundred miles from the headquarters for the Foundation Test Branch.

Specifically, the whistleblower alleged that Liebich had instructed Wiley and Wyllie to load steel beams and other state property, drive it to his Susanville property in a state vehicle, and use that state-owned metal to build a gate and other structures at Liebich's property. The steel was previously used in pile load tests and was later valued at about $10,000.[17]

The most troubling aspect of the relationship between Liebich and his subordinates is that it compromised all parties involved. Liebich had requested, perhaps even ordered, the technicians to move state property to his land, in a state vehicle and on state time. Liebich in turn had routinely approved fraudulent timesheets for those same employees, making it appear that the three were watching out for one another's criminal doings. State senator Mark DeSaulnier, whose committee would investigate this situation, said, "Criminal activity gave Wiles and maybe others the opinion that people in the (foundation testing) branch didn't need to do their jobs because their supervisor couldn't do anything about it."[18]

This symbiotic relationship became even more troubling when Caltrans and other officials began to learn that Wiles had fabricated data in his tests. As noted, the gamma gamma testing involved radiation, taken at various depths within a pile, to measure density and alert the state to any anomalies. The pile is poured with tubes in place, into which a technician can lower a gamma gamma device and record results at various depths in the pile. As early as September 2008 some within Caltrans began to suspect that Wiles was not doing his job. The gamma gamma tests for the La Sierra Avenue Bridge in Riverside had too little data, in the opinion of an engineer reviewing that data. The engineer asked Wiles to repeat the test. Wiles submitted a new set of data, which had clearly been copied from elsewhere, likely from tests on a different bridge or pile. Confronted with the suspect data, Wiles admitted that he had falsified the data but swore it was an isolated incident.

Knowledge that Wiles had falsified test results on this bridge raised two additional concerns. First, it was possible that Wiles was lying and had in fact falsified results on other bridges. More troubling still was the prospect that Wiles had falsified results from the giant Pier T-1 on the Bay Bridge, which was under construction at the time and for which Wiles had conducted gamma gamma testing.

As mentioned earlier in chapter 9, the piles for the SAS are steel pipes, which are filled with concrete for much of their depth. Tom Ho, vice-president at T. Y. Lin International, describes these piles: "The tower is fixed to the 6.5 m deep pile cap (consisting of a steel moment frame in-filled with concrete) and is supported on 13 2.5 m diameter steel shell pipe piles filled with concrete and socketed into rock."[19] The gamma gamma testing undertaken by Wiles involved the concrete in these piles beneath the pile cap for the SAS tower.[20]

The Federal Highway Administration in 2010 began its own investigation of the Foundation Test Branch work. Both Caltrans and the highway administration were alerted of questionable data on two additional structures: the foundation for an overhead sign in Oakland and a retaining wall in Los Angeles. Inspectors concluded that the data on these structures had been manipulated in the same manner as those data for the bridge in Riverside.

In November 2011 *Sacramento Bee* reporter Charles Piller began the first in a long series of articles on the falsified data and all the associated scandals, including the fraudulent overtime and stolen state property that began the investigation.[21] In November 2011 Piller reported that Wiles had worked on the Pier T-1 for the

Bay Bridge and questioned whether the safety of the concrete could be ensured. Wiles worked on the T-1 in 2006 and 2007, shortly before the state became suspicious of his practices. The BSA criticized Caltrans for allowing Wiles to have access to electronic gamma gamma files for eight months in 2008, after he was first suspected of falsification and before he was removed from testing duties: "This lengthy period of time provided Technician A [Wiles] with ample opportunity to further manipulate or delete those data files."[22]

The *Bee* articles gained national attention and resulted in numerous oversight hearings in the California legislature. Shortly after the first Piller article appeared, Caltrans fired both Wiles and Liebich.[23] The fact that Wiles had performed tests on the critical Pier T-1 caught the attention of politicians, including state senator DeSaulnier and Congresswoman Nancy Pelosi. In mid-November 2011 the Toll Bridge Program Oversight Committee convened an outside panel to determine whether the T-1 foundation had flaws or was unsafe.[24] The MTC expressed concern that Caltrans had known that Wiles had fabricated data but had not revealed that fact while T-1 was still under construction. Between 2009 and 2011 the tower itself was under construction, making it impossible to retest the T-1 foundation. Steve Heminger, executive director of the MTC, noted that Wiles was reprimanded for his falsification "over a year before the first steel was placed on top of this tower pier. Why that information was not conveyed to the relevant people running this program is something that simply has got to be fixed."[25]

In the following months, Caltrans, the MTC, and the Federal Highway Administration produced report after report for the legislature, detailing exactly what Wiles had done on the Bay Bridge. Wiles was involved in tests on seven of the thirteen piles on the T-1 pier. The integrity of those tests was questioned because Wiles had not verified the calibration of his device prior to conducting the tests, as required in his job description.[26]

In March 2012 a four-member panel hired by Caltrans to study the concrete at T-1 concluded that the pier was safe.[27] The *Sacramento Bee*, however, continued to pursue the story, using Caltrans tests and those conducted by Kiewit, the contractor. There followed a back-and-forth between Caltrans and the *Bee* over whether the concrete in T-1 was properly tested and therefore safe. In the meantime, construction continued on the metal tower for the SAS. Debate over the safety of the T-1 foundation continued until it was eclipsed by even more troubling developments with the metal of Pier E-2, just east of T-1, and the metal of the T-1 tower as well.

Bolts and Welds That Keep Breaking

In the months just before Labor Day 2013, when the new bridge was scheduled to open, Caltrans went public with information about two worrisome flaws in the metal for the SAS span. One problem concerned bolts on Pier E-2, which had been manufactured by an American steel company. The second had to do with the metal for the SAS tower and the steel box girders for the deck, all of which had been manufactured and assembled in China.

The bolt problems on E-2 were discovered in March 2013. Pier E-2 is in the Bay east of the main SAS tower and includes two tall concrete columns connected by a thick concrete transverse beam. The separate bridge decks connect with the transverse beam, one at either side. The bridge was designed with large shear panels between the deck girders and the transverse beam that could absorb the shock from an earthquake, rather than damaging the decks or the transverse beam. The intervening material, called *shear keys* and *bearings*, were held in place with wide (three-inch diameter) and long (up to twenty-four feet) bolts embedded in the concrete beam. The problem emerged when Caltrans tightened the bolts to specified tension. They tightened ninety-six bolts and thirty-two of them broke.

These failures suggested the shear keys and bearings could not be deemed functional. Furthermore, because the bolts were embedded in the concrete of the beam, the problem required a fix beyond simple replacement of the damaged pieces.[28] Ultimately, Caltrans would develop a saddle with steel tendons that would take the place of the bolts in holding the shear key and bearings in place.[29]

Questions about these bolts would persist well after the bridge opened and the saddle was installed. In December 2013 (about

Damaged bolts found on new Bay Bridge

At least 30 of the large bolts holding together the new eastern span of the Bay Bridge have snapped. The problem was first discovered at the easternmost end of the single-tower suspension.

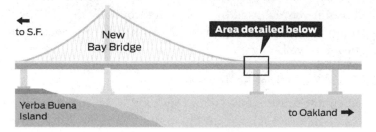

to S.F.

New
Bay Bridge

Area detailed below

Yerba Buena
Island

to Oakland ➡

Cross-section view

The roadbeds are being joined to a concrete cap beam using two types of devices, bearings and shear keys, designed to help the bridge withstand seismic forces. They are secured with 3-inch-diameter anchor rods ranging in length from 9 to 24 feet.

B **Bearing:** designed to support vertical forces

S **Shear key:** designed to resist side-to-side forces

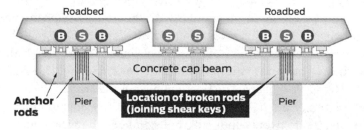

Roadbed

Roadbed

Concrete cap beam

Anchor rods | Pier

Location of broken rods (joining shear keys)

Pier

The rods, or bolts, are secured by placing nuts onto their threaded ends. A photograph provided by Caltrans shows a loosened nut, indicating that the bolt is damaged.

Source: Caltrans

Graphic by Todd Trumbull / The Chronicle

Diagram of broken bolts, *San Francisco Chronicle*, April 1, 2013. Courtesy of Carlos Avila Gonzalez/*San Francisco Chronicle*/Polaris.

four months after the bridge opened), Yun Chung and Lisa K. Thomas wrote a long and scathing critique of Caltrans' handling of the bolt problem. Chung was a retired metallurgist who had worked at various companies including Bechtel. Thomas was a materials engineer at Berkeley Research Company. Chung and Thomas concluded, "[the engineers at] Caltrans are not cognizant of metallurgical problems unique to these anchor bolts."[30] The authors believed that the bolts, manufactured by an Ohio-based company, were not built to withstand the sea air of the Bay and likely broke as a result of corrosion, a finding that offered little comfort about the durability of the hundreds of other bolts that did not break when first tested.

Meanwhile, weld issues on the main tower were made public only a few weeks before the larger bolt failures were observed. The weld problem occurred on the tower, just above the water line and above its connection to the troubled concrete pier.[31] Caltrans identified twenty instances in which long welds, each thirty-three feet long, cracked, for reasons that stymied the experts.

Like the bolt problem, the weld defect issue would remain a hot topic of public discussion, long after the bridge opened. In January 2014, about five months after the opening, the California State Senate Transportation and Housing Committee released a damning report that examined how Caltrans planned and built the new bridge. The report, "The San Francisco–Oakland Bay Bridge: Basic Reforms for the Future," focused chiefly on the lack of transparency in planning and building the bridge.[32] It used the weld problem as the chief case study in how Caltrans downplayed warnings about how the steel towers had been fabricated.

The tower contract was awarded to American Bridge/Fluor, but this American company subcontracted with the Chinese company ZPMC to fabricate the metal for the tower. Caltrans also hired a quality-assurance firm, MACTEC, to audit the work of ZPMC, to ensure the work matched specifications. The specifications called for no cracks in the welds, whether visible to the eye or identified through ultrasonic tests.

The weld problems were especially delicate and difficult to resolve because the work was being done in China. Although the various steel pieces were being fabricated and assembled outside

Shanghai, there were at least four groups of American quality-control people present. The contractor, American Bridge/Fluor, had representatives at the plant. Caltrans had quality-control people there most of the time. And Caltrans had commissioned a third party, MACTEC, to serve as an independent inspector. The MACTEC representative over most of the project was Jim Merrill. The Caltrans representatives for most of the project were Douglas Coe and Rick Morrow.

The first weld problems to be identified were on panels for the box girders; the panels were shipped unassembled to Oakland, where they were welded into the final box girder forms. In March 2008 Jim Merrill noticed so many cracked welds in the deck panels that he recommended all work be halted until ZPMC could develop a quality-control regimen. Instead, the Chinese company agreed to fix the weld problems, which worked to delay fabrication of new panels. As the construction fell behind, more and more cracks were identified. Both Merrill and Coe recommended rejecting suspect panels and requiring more-rigorous testing on the welds. In time, both were removed from the job; Coe was reassigned back to California, and Caltrans allowed the contract with Merrill's firm, MACTEC, to expire.

Caltrans ultimately devised two solutions to the cracked welds and the project falling behind schedule. It amended its contract with ZPMC to allow for a higher number of cracked welds. And it offered incentives to speed production, incentives that ultimately cost the state $250 million.[33]

The problems with the welds on the SAS deck called into question whether the 2013 bridge would perform as a lifeline structure in the event of an earthquake. It will be recalled that Caltrans' lifeline standard called for a bridge that could endure a maximum credible earthquake and be put into service within a day after such an event. It was the pursuit of a lifeline standard that caused the estimated cost of retrofitting the 1936 East Span to go up five-fold. And it was the guarantee that the 2013 bridge would perform as a lifeline structure that made replacement such an attractive option.

Studies on the SAS steel deck, however, caused many to question whether it would perform up to lifeline standards. In 2014 a *San Francisco Chronicle* reporter published notes from a meeting in 2010 in which Marwan Nader at T. Y. Lin warned Caltrans officials that the Chinese-made steel deck panels exhibited multiple deficiencies. The most difficult of these was the fact that the panels did not quite match up to one another, requiring additional welds to fill in gaps.[34] The article explored the implications of these faulty joints for the performance of the bridge as a lifeline:

> But several experts interviewed by The Chronicle said Caltrans's decision to accept the defective joints could undermine a key feature of the $6.4 billion span—its ability to be open to traffic soon after a quake.
>
> The Bay Bridge is designated as a "lifeline" structure—guaranteed to carry emergency traffic within a day of a major earthquake. If the welded connections holding the road-deck steel sections together are severely damaged, that's unlikely to happen, experts said. "This span is not robust to begin with," said Bob Bea, a UC Berkeley professor emeritus in civil engineering, "We can't predict exactly how the bridge could fail, but with this issue there is a high likelihood of trouble in its ability to serve as a lifeline structure."[35]

These safety concerns persisted, even after the bridge opened to traffic. In April 2014, six months after the bridge opened, the *Sacramento Bee*, which broke nearly every safety story about the bridge, reported that there was a troubling amount of rust developing at the anchorage blocks where the cables are attached to the roadway, at Pier W-2. There are 137 strands to the cable. Along most of the bridge, these strands are bound into a compact cable inside a cable cover. In the anchorage blocks, however, the strands splay out and each is attached to an anchor bar that attaches to a socket, where the threaded bar is held in place by a nut. This whole assembly is housed in a chamber (actually two chambers, one for each deck), measuring 130 feet long and 15 feet high. These chambers are meant to be watertight but the rods and strands apparently got wet, either during construction or through unexpected leakage.

How significant are the safety issues surrounding the 2013 bridge, particularly its SAS main span? It would be difficult to dismiss these concerns outright because they concern such critical bridge components: the foundation for the main pier, the steel for the pier cap, the integrity of the deck girder, and the cables themselves. But are the flaws so pronounced as to call into question the safety of the bridge? Steve Heminger, executive director of the MTC, believes the problems have been overstated. When the first batch of defective deck plates arrived, Heminger said, "Steel decks have cracks in 'em. The issue is not whether there's a crack there, it's whether it matters."[36] In a radio interview, Heminger spoke about the whole range of problems: "I have to say that most of the criticism we have heard lately about this bridge, I would call phantom problems. They're not real problems. They're just somebody digging deep enough and finding irregularities and blowing it out of proportion."[37]

Others are less convinced that the identified problems are not "real problems." In October 2013 the Cal Alumni Association published an article titled "Bridge Over Troubled Bolts: UC Berkeley Experts Raised Safety Concerns about New Bay Bridge."[38] The author of this article consulted various engineers associated with the campus. Retired engineering professor Bob Bea was pleased with the solution for the broken bolts but cautioned that "the problems with this structure are much more extensive than the seismic support bolts. (There are) corroded post tensioning tendons in the concrete girders (and) flawed welds in the suspension span support tower. (There are) lots of identified defects with high uncertainties concerning their effects on performance and safety."[39]

The harshest criticism, however, came from engineering professor Abolhassan Astaneh-Asl, who had recommended more than a decade earlier that the 1936 bridge could be safely retrofitted for a fraction of what the East Span replacement would cost. He laid out a litany of flaws:

> We know the steel they used has an issue with hydrogen embrittlement, which makes the bolts inadequate to the stresses they could face. There is also the matter of the 20

main welds that connect the legs of the tower to the tower's foundation. These are each about 30 foot long, and they have hundreds of visible cracks—and at least one of them is seven inches long. That's incredibly bad news. Cracks in welds are always a problem, but you usually can only detect them by sonic testing—and these can be seen with the naked eye.... There's no doubt in my mind that the old bridge is much, much safer than the new bridge. (The new span) should not be opened to the public. All the evidence that Caltrans has indicates the bridge will collapse when the Hayward Fault ruptures.[40]

The New Span Opens with Little Fanfare

The weld and broken bolt problems came to light just months before the planned opening of the new span on Labor Day 2013. Caltrans had originally planned a grand celebration with a partial marathon, fireworks, a concert, and other festivities. In spring and summer of that year, it was so unclear as to when the bridge might be opened that state officials called off the celebration.

Engineers were able to craft a short-term fix for the broken bolts; the more permanent saddle would not be installed until much later in 2013. The temporary fix enabled the agency to keep to its planned Labor Day opening, September 2, 2013. Local newscasts called the opening ceremony low key.[41] The governor was out of state and did not attend. Gavin Newsom, the lieutenant governor and former mayor of San Francisco, handled the ceremonial chain-cutting, using a blow torch in recreation of the 1936 opening of the larger Bay Bridge. He spoke briefly, saying he hoped the bridge would inspire "a generation to dream big dreams and do big things." Steve Heminger of the MTC sounded relieved: "Despite the journey's length, it has been completed before the arrival of our next big earthquake. And thank goodness for that." James Ghielmetti, a member of the California Transportation Commission, was less celebratory: "California must do a better job going forward on all of our public works projects."[42]

The California poet laureate, Jose Felipe Herrera, wrote a poem, called simply "Bay Bridge Inauguration Poem," and read it

Troubled bridge

Dueling designs

The bridge selection committee narrowed its choices to two: a cable-stayed tower design, which is widely used worldwide, and a self-anchored suspension span, the likes of which had never been tried on such a scale.

Cable-stayed tower

721 feet:
Height of tower needed to compete with SAS design

Height: 525 feet
Length: 1,607 feet

Symmetrical

◄— **902 feet** —►

Yerba Buena Island

Self-anchored suspension tower

Height: 525 feet
Length: 1,853 feet

Asymmetrical

◄— **1,263 feet** —►

Difficult bridge anchorages

The bridge's unusual design meant it had to be tilted and curved to meet the arc of the skyway. Unlike conventional suspension spans, the self-anchored design has under-deck anchorages, with its main cable looped over the tower in a figure-eight configuration. The complexity created delays and added $145 million in costs.

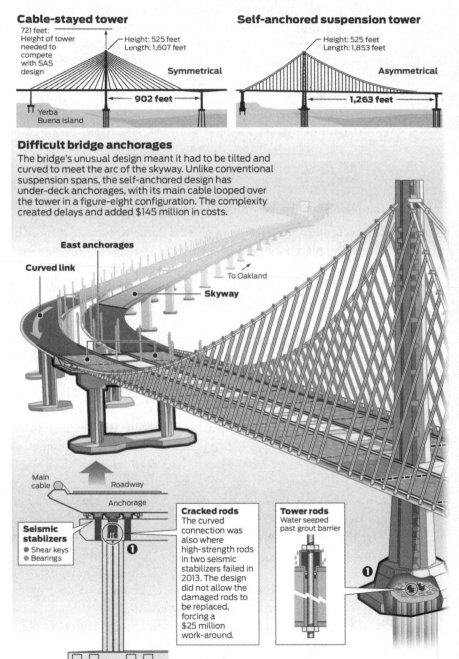

East anchorages

Curved link

To Oakland

Skyway

Main cable

Roadway

Anchorage

Seismic stablizers
● Shear keys
● Bearings

❶

Cracked rods
The curved connection was also where high-strength rods in two seismic stabilizers failed in 2013. The design did not allow the damaged rods to be replaced, forcing a $25 million work-around.

Tower rods
Water seeped past grout barrier

❶

Sources: Caltrans, T.Y. Lin International, American Bridge/Fluor, U.S. Department of Transportation (Federal Highway Administration)

Diagram of various problems with welds and broken bolts, *San Francisco Chronicle*, January 17, 2015. Courtesy of *San Francisco Chronicle*/Polaris

Issues with the self-anchored span

The selection of a self-anchored suspension span led to a number of problems when builders tried to translate its complex design into reality. These drove costs far higher than would have been expected on a cable-stayed bridge.

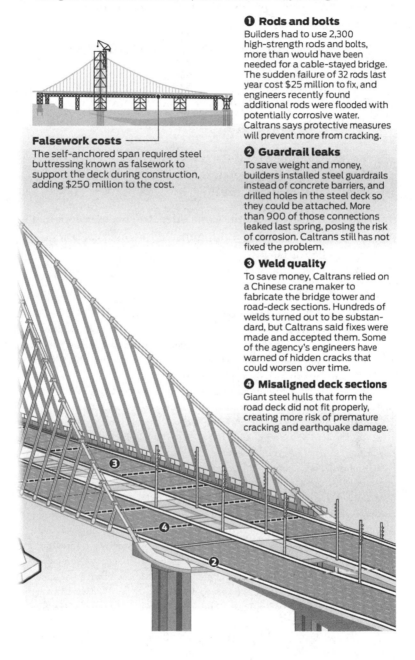

Falsework costs

The self-anchored span required steel buttressing known as falsework to support the deck during construction, adding $250 million to the cost.

❶ Rods and bolts

Builders had to use 2,300 high-strength rods and bolts, more than would have been needed for a cable-stayed bridge. The sudden failure of 32 rods last year cost $25 million to fix, and engineers recently found additional rods were flooded with potentially corrosive water. Caltrans says protective measures will prevent more from cracking.

❷ Guardrail leaks

To save weight and money, builders installed steel guardrails instead of concrete barriers, and drilled holes in the steel deck so they could be attached. More than 900 of those connections leaked last spring, posing the risk of corrosion. Caltrans still has not fixed the problem.

❸ Weld quality

To save money, Caltrans relied on a Chinese crane maker to fabricate the bridge tower and road-deck sections. Hundreds of welds turned out to be substandard, but Caltrans said fixes were made and accepted them. Some of the agency's engineers have warned of hidden cracks that could worsen over time.

❹ Misaligned deck sections

Giant steel hulls that form the road deck did not fit properly, creating more risk of premature cracking and earthquake damage.

at the celebration. (Two stanzas are quoted below.) Herrera's ode was for the workers who brought the challenging project to completion:

> Everything is open now spiritual inhalation of the Pacific
>   Rim
> Voyages migrations the conversations of generations Viva!
> The workers applaud now iron-workers painters welders
>   planners
>
> Architects engineers laborers drivers Viva!
> Lifters callers crane operators Viva!
> Cement mixers cable threaders Viva![43]

And with those festivities concluded, the bridge reopened in time for a busy September 3 commute, following total bridge closure for the Labor Day weekend.

Notes

1. The design of the bridge is detailed in two highly readable sources. The first is an article written by Tom Ho, Vice-President at T. Y. Lin International, who was actively involved in the design. "The Design and Construction of the New San Francisco–Oakland Bay Bridge (SFOBB) East Span." At MTC Library, Oakland, CA. The other is MacDonald, *Bay Bridge*.

2. "After 12 Years, Groundbreaking Gets Bridge Project Under Way," *Oakland Tribune*, January 30, 2002, 1.

3. Requests for bids on the SAS would not be released for another year.

4. California Research Bureau, "Timeline of the San Francisco–Oakland Bay Bridge Seismic Retrofit: Milestones in Decision-Making, Financing, and Construction," Sacramento, CA, December 2004. 30.

5. Ibid., 31, 32.

6. Larry Gerston and Terry Christensen, *Recall: California's Political Earthquake* (Amonk, NY: M. E. Sharpe, 2004).

7. Will Kempton, Governor Schwarzenegger's director at Caltrans, reiterated a point often made by Caltrans officials: that the concrete viaduct design was better understood and thus much easier to build. "There are some challengers [to the skyway design]. But there are few unknowns with the skyway. This is a much simpler kind of design, and we are very familiar with this type of work." Kempton quoted in Frick, "The Making and Un-Making of the San Francisco–Oakland Bay Bridge," 21.

8. "Simpler? Definitely. Cheaper? Maybe." *San Francisco Chronicle*, December 11, 2004.

9. McClintock quoted in Frick, "The Making and Un-Making of the San Francisco–Oakland Bay Bridge," 187.

10. LAO, "Hard Decisions before the Legislature: Toll Bridge Seismic Retrofit," Sacramento, CA, January 24, 2005.

11. Ibid., 13.

12. Frick, "The Making and Un-Making of the San Francisco–Oakland Bay Bridge," 190.

13. Ibid., 191.

14. "San Francisco–Oakland Bay Bridge Self-Anchored Suspension (SAS) Span Contract Awarded," Caltrans Press Release, April 18, 2006.

15. BSA, "Caltrans Employees Engaged in Inexcusable Neglect of Duty, Received Overpayment for Overtime, Falsified Test Data, and Misappropriated State Property," Report 2009-0640, 2009, p. 6. The BSA report identifies the two as Technician A and Technician B. Wiles' name became public when he was fired.

16. Ibid, 7.

17. Ibid., 20.

18. DeSaulnier quoted in "Lawmaker: Report May Help Explain Testing Troubles," *Sacramento Bee*, November 27, 2011. In time, Wiles and Liebich were fired while Wyllie was suspended for forty-five days. Wyllie's suspension was later reduced to ten days and Wiles was allowed to retire.

19. Ho, "Design and Construction." N.p.

20. An excellent summary of these events is provided in a report to the California State Senate Transportation Committee, "Department of Transportation: Bridge Foundation Inspection Practices," November 22, 2011. Sacramento, CA.

21. The story was especially interesting in 2011 when Wiles was charged in San Joaquin County with felony sex crimes against a child. "Questions Raised on Bay Bridge Structural Tests," *Sacramento Bee*, November 13, 2011.

22. BSA, "Caltrans Employees Engaged in Inexcusable Neglect of Duty, Received Overpayment for Overtime, Falsified Test Data, and Misappropriated State Property," Report 2009-0640, 2009, p. 13.

23. Shortly after he was fired, Wiles was able to retire, preserving his pension. As of this writing, Liebich's status is still being contested.

24. "Panel to Check Tower Safety," *Sacramento Bee*, November 16, 2011.

25. "Bay Area Panel Criticizes Caltrans over Fired Worker," *Sacramento Bee*, November 17, 2011.

26. "Caltrans Releases Data on Troubles in Bridge Test Unit," *Sacramento Bee*, November 22, 2011.

27. "Foundation of New Bridge is Safe, Panel Finds," *Sacramento Bee*, March 24, 2012.

28. "Bridge Rods Tests Detected an Issue," *San Francisco Chronicle*, April 2, 2013.

29. These bolts were manufactured in two pours in 2008 and 2010. The 2008 bolts failed. Caltrans, "Briefing on E2 Anchor Bolts—April 24, 2013,"

http://www.baybridgeinfo.org/sites/default/files/pdf/E2%20Anchor%20
Rods%20for%20BATA%20April%2024%202013%20Final.pdf

30. "Engineers' Dissent Blasts Bridge Safety Report," *Sacramento Bee*, December 8, 2013.

31. "Caltrans is 'On Top of the Problem,' Says Issue Doesn't Affect Span Safety," *Sacramento Bee*, May 2, 2013.

32. California State Senate Transportation and Housing Committee. "The San Francisco–Oakland Bay Bridge: Basic Reforms for the Future," Sacramento, CA January 2014.

33. The history of this contract is outlined in "Doubts Persist on Bay Bridge Job: Caltrans' Drive for Speed, Savings Overrode Experts' Safety Concerns," a long Charles Piller article in the *Sacramento Bee*, June 8, 2014.

34. "Bay Bridge Designer Warned Caltrans in 2010 of Weld Weakness," *San Francisco Chronicle*, February 25, 2014.

35. Ibid.

36. Heminger quoted in "Doubts Persist on Bay Bridge Job: Caltrans' Drive for Speed, Savings Overrode Experts' Safety Concerns," *Sacramento Bee*, June 8, 2014.

37. Heminger quoted in PBS Newshour, "Broken Bolts Is Latest Woe for Late, Overbudget and Earthquake-Prone Bay Bridge," transcript, August 12, 2013.

38. Glen Martin, "Bridge Over Troubled Bolts: UC Berkeley Experts Raised Safety Concerns about New Bay Bridge," Cal Alumni Association, October 27, 2013.

39. Ibid., 3.

40. Ibid., 4.

41. "New Bay Bridge Eastern Span Opens after Low-Key Afternoon Ceremony," CBS Bay Area, September 2, 2013.

42. Ibid.

43. Juan Felipe Herrera, "Bay Bridge Inauguration Poem," University of California–Riverside, "California Poet Laureate Celebrates Bay Bridge," August 28, 2013.

Conclusion

In 2003 Alan Altshuler and David Luberoff of the Kennedy School of Government at Harvard University published an important study, *Mega-Projects: The Changing Politics of Urban Public Investment*.[1] They analyzed dozens of over-budget and behind-schedule megaprojects in the United States in recent decades. Their analysis, however, does not mention the East Span project, which was under construction as they went to press but for which the true dimensions of delays and costs were not yet fully understood.

In another important study in 2003, Bent Flyvjberg, Mette K. Skampris Holm, and Soren Buhl published the results of an intensive investigation of 258 large transportation projects from around the world.[2] Flyvjberg and colleagues argued that cost overruns are common, and are almost always present in dealing with large transportation projects. The authors note, however, that spectacular cost overruns such as those experienced with the East Span are rare indeed, exceeding the norm many times over. Of the 258 projects they analyzed, nine of ten experienced cost overruns. These overruns, however, averaged only 28 percent.

Although Altshuler and Luberoff analyzed dozens of large undertakings, they focused in particular on two highly publicized projects that were completed by the time of their analysis—the Central Artery/Tunnel, or Big Dig, in Boston; and the new Denver International Airport outside Denver. The Big Dig was estimated to cost $3.7 billion but ultimately cost more than $15 billion, in constant 2002 values. The cost of the Denver International Airport rose from an estimate of $1 billion to $3 billion. The Bay Bridge East Span was estimated to cost $1 billion at the outset but ultimately cost $6.4 billion.[3] It is possible that the East Span and the Big Dig share the American if not the world record for the highest percentage of cost overrun for recently completed megaprojects.

A case could be made that the East Span was also the world record holder among megaprojects for having the lowest "benefit-cost ratio."[4] The literature of megaprojects emphasizes the degree to which political and business leaders are attracted to these very large but risky projects for the degree to which they can transform a city, state, or region. Flyvjberg, for example, refers to the attraction of megaprojects as "The Great War of Independence from Space," projects that can free an economy and a people from the constraints of space.[5]

Although their costs were high, the Denver International Airport and the Big Dig delivered impressive benefits. The airport gave Denver the largest airport in the United States and one of the largest in the world. The Big Dig transformed an entire neighborhood of Boston and vastly improved freeway-to-freeway connections. It greatly facilitated the movement of goods and people within the downtown and to the airport and removed an elevated freeway commonly viewed as an eyesore and a barrier between neighborhoods. It also opened land for the Rose Kennedy Greenway, a linear park that replaces the former elevated freeway.

The 2013 East Span is notable for how little it actually changed things in the Bay Area. It did not increase capacity on the perennially clogged Bay Bridge. It might or might not be a better-looking bridge than the one it replaced; the aesthetics of the two bridges are difficult to compare. From the outset, Caltrans sold the project as necessary for the safety of the public, a conclusion based on an assumption the old bridge could not be retrofitted to an acceptable level of safety. Not everyone agrees with that assumption. Professor Astaneh-Asl of Berkeley argued that Caltrans had "been telling everyone who will listen that the old bridge is unsafe, and now it's widely accepted. That's simply not true."[6] Even if the old bridge were unsafe, many disagree as to whether the new bridge is safer than the one it replaced. The only clear benefit from the East Span replacement is measured in safety and in life-cycle costs, especially maintenance. But even the claim of reduced future maintenance costs cannot be assumed to be true. In 2014, for example, Caltrans intended to spend $8 million on the East Span to test the remaining large bolts to see whether it should place more saddles, or apply some other fix, to compensate for

Rose Kennedy Greenway, Boston. Photo by author.

the weakness of those bolts. Other perceived safety issues such as the rusting of the cable strands will also surely add to the life-cycle costs of the 2013 span.

Of the various measures we could use, the benefit-cost ratio makes the largest distinction between the 1936 and 2013 versions of the Bay Bridge. On the cost side of the equation, the 1936 bridge was a bargain. The $77 million spent on the bridge in 1936 has a 2013 value of just over $1.2 billion. That was for the bridge and the Transbay Terminal and major approach work. The $6.4 billion for the 2013 East Bay span is at least ten times more expensive, especially figuring the work involved less than half the bridge built in 1936.[7] On the benefit side of the equation, the 1936 bridge accomplished what political and business leaders hope to see from megaprojects: it transformed the space of the Bay Area. Nothing about transportation in the Bay Area, whether on land or sea, would ever be the same after the Bay Bridge was built. By contrast, the 2013 bridge does little that the 1936 bridge did not do. It did not increase the capacity except for the addition of a bicycle and pedestrian lane, linking the East Bay with Yerba Buena Island but not with San Francisco. Built at an enormous cost and with small benefits, the 2013 bridge was no bargain.

We have nearly eighty years of perspective on the performance of the 1936 bridge but only a few years of experience with the 2013 bridge. It is admittedly premature to compare what the two contributed to the economy, society, and transportation network of the region. It is not too early, however, to consider the processes through which the two bridges were approved, designed, and built. This comparison will point to the effectiveness of the process for the 1936 bridge and the ineffectiveness of the process for the 2013 bridge. This comparison is neither intended to criticize those involved with the 2013 structure nor to praise those who toiled in the 1930s. Rather, it is to draw some conclusions that might be of use to those who plan megaprojects in the future. What can we learn from two generations of megaprojects on the same alignment that might help any public agency contemplating the construction of a behemoth megaproject?

The lessons are many but five general maxims summarize the difference between the two projects, indicating why one worked well and the other did not.

1. Build broad consensus about the purpose and need for the project.

The term *purpose and need* has come into popular use in recent decades with regard to federal planning and environmental documents for transportation projects.[8] The concept, however, is as old as the building of public works. What is the purpose of the project? In other words, what is it designed to accomplish? And is there a demonstrable need for the project?

Bay Area business and political leaders campaigned aggressively throughout the 1920s for constructing a bridge between San Francisco and the East Bay. San Francisco officials took the lead but the effort was strongly backed by business and political leaders in the East Bay as well. All indications are that the bridge effort was supported by the general citizenry as well, particularly the tens of thousands who commuted between their homes in the East Bay and their jobs in San Francisco.

This long campaign allowed Bay Area leaders to develop a rational and convincing case that the bridge had a clear purpose and that there was a tangible need for it. The purpose was straightforward: to link the highway and rail systems on the East Bay with the highway and rail systems in San Francisco. The need could be easily proven by counting the number of passenger ferry fares and the number of automobile ferry crossings, something that was accomplished during the planning process in the 1920s and that produced numbers to support taking on bonded indebtedness equal to the fares the bridge could support.

The 2013 bridge by contrast suffered because there was no consensus on either the purpose or the need to build a new structure between Yerba Buena Island and Oakland. There was consensus that the bridge should be safe and able to withstand a major earthquake. There was no consensus, however, that it was necessary to build a new bridge to accomplish that goal. It might have been possible for Caltrans to make a convincing case for a replacement structure, given enough time and evidence. In actual practice, however, the agency made little effort to convince political leaders or the public of the pressing need for demolishing the old bridge and building a new one.

The major difference between the 1936 and 2013 experiences, in terms of justifying a purpose and need, is that the 1936 consensus arose from the bottom up and the 2013 decision to replace the East Span came from the top down. By the time the state of California decided to build this bridge in 1931, Bay Area political and business leaders had campaigned for at least a decade in favor of constructing a transbay crossing. While the effort was championed by men like M. M. O'Shaughnessy and Leland Cutler, there is also strong evidence the campaign was favored by the general public.

By contrast, the decision to replace the East Span was made with little direct involvement by the general public, politicians, or business leaders. Indeed, it is difficult to say exactly how, why, and by whom the decision was made to build a new East Span. In the years just after the 1989 earthquake, all attention by Caltrans and others was focused on retrofitting the 1936 bridge. And then, at some point in 1996, Caltrans began to argue that it was necessary to build a new structure at the East Span. Behind the scenes, state officials adopted a lifeline level of safety, one that ensured the bridge would be available one day after a massive earthquake.

No doubt there were intense debates within Caltrans and possibly among Caltrans and other state and local officials about the replacement versus retrofit question. But there was little that was said in a public forum and there certainly was nothing like the locally led campaign that preceded the 1936 structure.

Because the proposal came almost exclusively from Caltrans, the public and the political leaders were less forgiving than they might have been when things began to go wrong with the project. When the MTC took a more active role in planning the project, it too came to own problems associated with the project. These problems—massive cost overruns, long construction delays, scary construction flaws—might have happened, even if the public had been strongly behind the project. Lacking broad support, however, Caltrans was isolated when the project began to fail. The frustration and finger-pointing was directed almost exclusively at Caltrans. Some sense of that isolation is captured in the scathing comments of Senator Don Perata, a Democrat: "The same agency that botched the last estimate is the same agency recommending we build the skyway, saying it won't take any longer and promising it will save money. I'm not sure there's a lot of confidence in Caltrans there."[9] Senator Tom McClintock, a Republican, joined in: "It's the biggest fiasco in California transportation history. This was a simple retrofit of that bridge that has been botched beyond anyone's wildest imagination."[10]

2. Let political people make political decisions and let technical people make technical decisions.

In 1929 and 1930 President Herbert Hoover and Governor C. C. Young created a unique and effective method for planning a megaproject. For Hoover and Young, the decision was not whether the Bay Bridge should be a suspension or a cantilever structure, which is a technical issue they decided to leave for technical people to decide. Hoover and Young were political people at the highest level, although Hoover was also an engineer, which might have influenced his instinct to leave technical matters to engineers. When they convened the Hoover–Young Commission, the president and governor assembled an august body of experts to advise them on how to make decisions that, while founded in technical considerations, were uniquely in the province of high-level elected officials: Should the state of California and the United States commit many millions of dollars to this megaproject?

Even the Hoover–Young Commission itself comprised political people as well as technical people who were known and trusted by the president and the governor. One could argue that even the military members of the commission were of such high rank—admirals and generals all—that they could be seen as political people within the specifically military context.

The commission, clearly a political body, turned to technicians (engineers) at the division of highways for technical guidance. Charles Purcell and Charles Andrew were dedicated public servants but politically savvy enough to recognize the political firepower represented by members of the commission. They were cautious and smart enough to provide only the best cost estimates and other technical advice to commission members. The commission was inclined to defer to Purcell and Andrew the analysis of technical matters, from cost estimates to foundation studies. This near-total delegation of authority for technical analysis was built on trust. If the political leadership of the commission had suspected Purcell and Andrew of providing misleading information, however, it is likely that trust would have evaporated and the delegation of power with it.

Ultimately, the Hoover–Young Commission accepted the technical analysis and recommendations of Purcell and Andrew as well as dozens of private consultants whose work was reviewed and approved by the state workers. The big decision—whether the state of California should commit itself to this massive and expensive project—was made by political people, acting on the advice of technical experts.

During the design of the bridge, 1931–33, and its construction, 1933–36, thousands of decisions great and small were made by a tight cadre of highly technical people. Purcell and Andrew hired Glen Woodruff and brought in five consulting engineers, drawn from the ranks of the best-known and most-respected engineers in the world. The Board of Consulting Engineers was not there for window dressing or to rubber stamp decisions made by the Bay Bridge Division. The Bay Bridge Division did the heavy lifting in preparing construction documents, making routine calculations, and so forth. When there was a major decision to be made—the bridge type for the west crossing, how to build foundations of the east crossing, and so forth—the Bay Bridge Division turned to the Board of Consulting Engineers.

What President Hoover and Governor Young accomplished was a strong buy-in by all concerned parties that the bridge should be built and should be financed in a particular manner— through self-liquidating revenue bonds. Beyond that, they and the members of the commission they appointed left the details to the bridge people. It turned out that the bridge people were capable and wise enough to stay within budget.

The 2013 bridge experience was, in many respects, the reverse of what happened in 1936. Engineers and planners at Caltrans, attempting to ensure lifeline standards could be met, concluded it was more cost-effective to replace than to repair the eastern half of the bridge. It was necessary, of course, for legislative leaders, the governor, and local officials to endorse the strategy. These approvals were gained, however, very late in the process, following more than a decade of studies by Caltrans. The technical people at Caltrans made the decision that the bridge should be replaced and asked political leaders to endorse their conclusions. There was never a question that Caltrans owned the idea of replacing the East Span.

Conversely, the technical decisions about the new span— north or south alignment, skyway, cable-stayed, or SAS—were pulled away from Caltrans and filtered through an elaborate and painfully slow process of public hearings and advisory panel built on advisory panel. It was as if the 1936 model had been stood on its head, with the essentially political decisions to commit the resources of the state made by the technical people, and the essentially technical decisions of bridge design made by political bodies or through a political process.

In retrospect, both sides of the 2013 model produced mistakes. The decision to commit the state of California to a multi-billion-dollar project was best made after proper deliberation by the political bodies of the state, including the governor and legislature, with full buy-in from local political leaders, recognizing that most of the funding would come from Bay Area sources. Those political leaders needed and deserved the best and most-reliable cost estimation available. State transportation officials made little effort to vet the replacement decision through political leaders before going public with various technical studies that supported the replacement option. And, we can conclude in hindsight, the cost estimates they provided to political leaders were so off base as to be fundamentally misleading.

Conversely, it was a mistake to entrust bridge type selection to political leaders. It is inconceivable that Charles Purcell or Ralph Modjeski would have consulted the mayors of San Francisco and Oakland on whether to build a continuous suspension bridge or a center anchorage structure for the West Bay crossing or a tied arch or a cantilever for the East Bay. Neither was it a good idea for Caltrans or the MTC to leave the selection of a bridge type to citizens' advisory panels. For example, it can be seen in retrospect that nearly all of the construction problems associated with the East Span project were directly linked to the single tower SAS span, a largely experimental design that was troublesome for the design engineers, the construction firms, and the firms that supplied the steel and concrete for it. Few technical people supported the SAS design; it was selected chiefly by advisory panels established by local interests. Take away the SAS and many of the safety issues that haunt the bridge would have disappeared.

And the matter did not go away when the SAS was first selected. When the cost estimation errors finally came to light, political leaders at all levels were forced to address the issue of whether the SAS was worth the cost and predicted buildability issues. Caltrans attempted to reestablish technical control over the bridge type decision, arguing that the SAS had been a terrible mistake. By then, however, the genie was out of the bottle. The decision to stick with the SAS design was once again a political choice, made by the Bay Area leaders whose constituents were going to pay for it. In retrospect, one can conclude that it was a bad decision the first time and a bad decision the second time. The fault was not with the political leaders making the decision but in the decision-making process that assigned this highly technical matter to the leaders' province.

In 2005 Senator Don Perata, a powerhouse in East Bay politics, lamented the upside-down nature of the planning process. On delivering a compromise to make up for budget overruns, Perata noted, "Maybe this will get the thing off dead center. We've been arguing about silly things. Legislators ought not to be debating the design. We should figure out the financing and leave it to Caltrans to get it built."[11]

3. A megaproject will succeed or fail based on the quality of cost estimation.

The cost estimation for the 1936 bridge followed an unusual but quite successful process. The economic studies conducted as part of the Hoover–Young Commission deliberations established a ceiling of $77 million (about $1.2 billion in 2013 values) that could be supported by toll revenues while maintaining a self-liquidating status for the revenue bonds, a requirement of the Reconstruction Finance Corporation, which financed the bonds. That was all that it was prepared to lend and it was unlikely that private parties would lend anything more. The $77 million figure became a budget for the bridge, one that the Bay Bridge Division and its consulting engineers could not exceed. The bridge was ultimately built with a little less money than was budgeted.

Under the circumstances, there was little reason to doubt the sincerity or accuracy of the cost estimates produced by the Bay Bridge Division. The bonding limit enforced a rigor on cost estimating and produced excellent results.

By comparison, cost estimation for the 2013 bridge was dramatically off the mark. Altshuler and Flyvjberg dedicate large sections of their analysis to the issue of cost underestimation. Both note that megaprojects are usually underestimated; Flyvjberg concludes that 90 percent of large projects he studied were underestimated.[12] These underestimates were typically in the 30 percent, not 600 percent, range. But even these relatively minor underestimations are so common that neither Altshuler nor Flyvjberg believe this pattern to be the result of miscalculation alone. Rather, Altshuler notes that most observers attribute the pattern to "tactics in the pursuit of project approvals rather than innocent mistakes."[13] Flyvjberg is more direct in his criticism: "The cost estimates used in public debates, media coverage, and decision making for transport infrastructure are systematically and significantly deceptive."[14] Altshuler also quotes Martin Wachs with an even more damning analysis of cost overruns, in his case for transit projects seeking federal approvals: "In case after case, planners, engineers, and economists have told me they had to 'revise' their forecasts many times because they failed to satisfy their superiors. The forecasts had to be 'cooked' in order to produce numbers that were dramatic enough to gain federal support for projects whether or not they could be justified on technical grounds."[15]

The the East Span, then, was certainly not the first or the only megaproject to be approved on the basis of cost underestimation. Altshuler observes that the long history of underestimation had taken a toll on public confidence. "In our view, consistent underestimation is an example of the 'tragedy of the commons.' It corrodes public confidence in government overall, and especially in proposals with long time frames, even as it helps advance specific projects."[16]

California had prior to the East Span been spared experiences with systematic underestimation. Altshuler analyzes the Century Freeway, built in Los Angeles in the late 1970s, that ballooned from an original estimate of $500 million to about $1.6 billion. Much of the additional costs, however, can be attributed to a court settlement that forced Caltrans to provide thousands of low-cost housing units to replace those displaced by the freeway.[17]

With respect to the 2013 Bay Bridge, the political leadership in California quickly became disillusioned as the cost estimates mushroomed year after year in increments of $1 billion each. One measure of this disillusionment is the reaction of a key Democratic leader from the Bay Area: Senator Mark DeSaulnier, chair of the Senate Transportation Commission. On January 23, 2014, Senator DeSaulnier made the following statement, with respect to hearings he planned to hold on how the bridge was managed:

> I want to thank the administration for making many officials and documents available during our investigation into the development and construction of the Eastern Span of the Bay Bridge. I am convinced that the Senate Transportation and Housing Committee and administration officials

want the same thing—to create a more transparent, accountable Caltrans. I think that the testimony at tomorrow's hearing will illustrate the need to enact reforms that will begin to change the culture at Caltrans, making the department more accessible and open to the public. We need Caltrans to be more responsive to its clients—the taxpayers. It is imperative that the department regain the public trust, as we continue to invest in necessary public works projects to improve California's infrastructure.[18]

After the initial cost estimates were shown to be off the mark, Caltrans suffered in terms of support among elected officials, particularly those from the Bay Area, who represented constituents who were asked to increase their bridge tolls from $1.00 to $6.00, chiefly to pay off the Bay Bridge cost overruns. Caltrans was not responsible for all factors that caused the cost of the bridge to rise. The decision to build the SAS span, for example, accounted for a substantial part of those increases. The ineptitude of the Chinese steel manufacturers also contributed to it. But Caltrans could never escape the conclusion by political leaders that they had been sold a bridge that was supposed to cost $1 billion and ultimately cost six or more times that. Caltrans made, and Caltrans owned, that cost estimate and the angst that followed.

4. If an agency underestimates costs, it should make certain there is a reliable basis to fund cost overruns.

If there was a saving grace for the 2013 bridge, it was that political and technical people had a solution to solve cost overruns: raise bridge tolls. When the decision was made to replace the East Bay crossing, the toll for the Bay Bridge was $1.00. Today, the toll is $6.00 in peak times and $5.00 at other times. This 600 percent increase roughly corresponds to the increase in the estimate for the replacement bridge costs. The bridge tolls, in other words, provided a cushion that allowed for bridge construction, despite overruns.

This comfort level was not available to the designers of the 1936 span. They were instructed from the outset that there was an outside limit to the cost for the bridge and any cost above that limit might destroy the good faith and credit of the state of

California. The 1936 understanding of a self-liquidating bond was different from that perceived by Caltrans and political leaders who approved the 2013 structure. Everyone involved in the 1936 bridge understood that there were bonds to be issued to pay for construction and that the tolls would need to cover the total expense of those bonds. The total expense of the 2013 bridge bonds, including interest payments, is estimated to be $13 billion, something the daily tolls of the Bay Bridge will be many decades in paying off.[19]

But at least Caltrans and political leaders in 2013 had this option available to them. The designers of the 1936 Bay Bridge did not, and neither did the planners for the Big Dig in Boston. The 1936 design team accepted as a given that the $77 million available to them was all they would ever get and that there would never be any type of augmentation. The Big Dig designers understood that there would be implications for cost overruns but largely ignored those warnings and left others to figure out how to pay for the huge overruns. The residual debt is derisively called the "Big Dig Debt."[20]

In 2005 the bids for the SAS work came in so far beyond Caltrans' estimates that state and Bay Area leaders were forced to reconsider the entire program. For nearly a year, predominantly Democratic political leaders from the Bay Area faced off against Republican Governor Arnold Schwarzenegger regarding how to pay for these overruns. The governor agreed the state could pay for the work but only if the design was the simpler and cheaper skyway. An internal review team suggested building the cable-stayed bridge as a middle ground that was visually dramatic but not as difficult to construct as the SAS. Bay Area leaders were disinclined to reopen the already painful design process and were in any event unhappy with the skyway design. This stalemate persisted for months until Bay Area leaders conceded the point that there was no way to build a good-looking bridge without raising tolls.

5. Do not allow technology to get ahead of functionality.

One of the most perceptive points made by Karen Frick in her analysis of the 2013 bridge is her use of the concept of the "technological sublime," a phrase she borrows from historian Leo Marx's classic, *The Machine in the Garden*. Marx uses this concept to describe America's fascination with technological advancement. Frick uses this concept to describe the drive of Bay Area leaders to ensure the new bridge would have a signature span, or, as Mayor Jerry Brown of Oakland phrased it, a bridge specific to the site, not one that "could be just anywhere."[21]

Those discussions led Bay Area leaders to select an exotic bridge type, a selection that many would regret because it led to long delays, cost overruns, and serious construction issues. In the months of debates over the bridge type, architects, engineers, and political leaders did not overtly seek out the most exotic and riskiest bridge type. Rather, the principal advisory panel, the EDAP, and other advisory boards debated a balance between aesthetics and functionality. They were told repeatedly that the concrete box girder viaduct, or skyway, was the most functional type for this crossing. It was also, in the opinion of most people, the least attractive of various options. By contrast, the single tower SAS design was, in the opinion of a slim majority of EDAP members, the best-looking bridge for the crossing. They were warned, however, that it posed grave risks for delays, cost overruns, and safety concerns. The panelists knowingly selected the most attractive but riskiest option.

To understand the nature of the risk taken in this decision, it is useful to compare the history of the design of the 1936 bridge with that of the 2013 bridge. The designers of the 1936 bridge wrestled with this aesthetics–functionality balance in deciding what to do with the suspension spans on the West Bay crossing. After exploring various alternatives, the final choice was between two options. One was a conventional suspension bridge (two towers and two land-based anchorages) but with gigantic spans, far exceeding anything built before. The other option (and the one that was built) involved a double suspension bridge, with four towers and three anchorages, two on land and one in the water.

The giant conventional suspension span was ultimately rejected by the panel of engineers because they feared the technology and because it was more expensive to build. Daniel Moran (a member of the Board of Consulting Engineers) supported the option chiefly on the basis of its aesthetics. Moran wrote an impassioned letter to the rest of the board, urging adoption of the single suspension design: "We would further call the attention to the Board to the greater advantages, to the cities of San Francisco and Oakland, of a single span design; first, it would provide the best possible water way for shipping and; second, because it would undoubtedly create a bridge which architecturally and spectacularly would appeal to the civic pride of both Cities, and would attract and interest all of the surrounding district."[22]

Moran argued further that to build the double bridge "would also indicate that the design was one adopted for economic reasons rather than for reasons based upon harbor requirements plus architectural requirements."[23] Moran's arguments could have been used almost verbatim by those who opposed building a skyway in the early twenty-first century!

Although Moran suggested the double bridge was favored for budgetary reasons, the records of the Board of Consulting Engineers document that the board majority rejected the single bridge because they were concerned it might be risky to build and ultimately unsafe at this seismically active and wind-swept site. Of the board members, only Modjeski and Moisseiff had extensive experience in building suspension bridges. And neither was entirely risk-averse. Indeed, even the selected double bridge design was risky because it had never been tried before. Less than a decade after the Bay Bridge was built, Moisseiff took one of the great gambles in bridge-building history, building a suspension bridge at Tacoma Narrows without the conventional stiffening truss at the deck level. The theory that the stiffening truss was unnecessary was proved tragically wrong when the deck swayed badly in the wind before finally collapsing due to aeroelastic flutter.

The single bridge versus double bridge debate divided the Board of Consulting Engineers more than any other issue. Moisseiff also supported the single bridge design, downplaying concern by Modjeski and Glen Woodruff that it would be difficult to design a stiffening truss able to withstand wind and seismic stresses at this crossing. In the end, Modjeski, Woodruff, and Purcell supported the double bridge design as the less risky of two challenging options. In addition, Modjeski disagreed with Moran that the double bridge design was inferior from an aesthetic standpoint. He wrote to Purcell, expressing his opinion that the twin-bridge plan was superior "from the standpoint of economy as well as aesthetics."[24]

The debates leading to the 2013 SAS design are notable for the extent to which EDAP members ignored the risks associated with the single-tower SAS. T. Y. Lin, one of the most respected bridge engineers in the world, was on the EDAP and argued forcefully that the SAS was folly. Jerry Brown, then mayor of Oakland, noted, "T. Y. Lin, who submitted another design for the bridge, told me before he died that constructing the self-anchored, one-tower suspension bridge would be an engineering nightmare. Cost overruns were inevitable from day one."[25] Professor Astaneh-Asl similarly expressed the opinion that the EDAP had selected the riskiest possible design, not to mention the design that was the most expensive and most difficult to build. The EDAP and the rest of the local decision-making apparatus elevated aesthetics to the highest level possible, essentially ignoring all other considerations, including cost and buildability.

Perhaps the most frustrating aspect of this aesthetics-first approach was that there was never unanimity that the SAS design was the most pleasing solution to the crossing. The EDAP was itself divided, favoring the SAS over a cable-stayed structure by a vote of twelve to seven. The SAS was opposed by Alan Hess and John King, the two most respected architectural critics in the Bay Area. Alan Hess favored the skyway: "The fact is that a bold engineering statement simply isn't needed. The skyway proposed initially last year was a simple thread rising with the least amount of fuss and the most slender profile from the Oakland mudflats to Yerba Buena tunnel."[26] John King, architectural critic for the *San Francisco Chronicle*, wrote of the SAS tower, after having visited it as it neared completion, "Yet even as I marveled, I wondered about our priorities. The beauty of the Golden Gate Bridge, or this one's western span, is inseparable from function: The capabilities of an age are focused on the task at hand, romance the outgrowth of rigor. Not so with the new eastern span, where our tower-to-come is an architectural affectation."[27]

King's comment about the failure of the SAS is also a comment about the success of the 1936 bridge. Its designers were not people who were unconcerned about aesthetics. True, they were also concerned about cost and buildability, a trait rare enough among the designers of modern megaprojects. They solved problems, to use Hess' phrase, with the least amount of fuss. The beauty of their work, to use King's phrase, is inseparable from function and "the outgrowth of rigor."

The 1936 bridge, even the much-maligned cantilever and truss East Bay crossing, was beautiful for its economy and functionality. The designers of that bridge did not allow aesthetics to get ahead of technology. Rather, they created aesthetic appeal in the way they used technology; they allowed technology to reveal its own beauty. And that simple fact comes close to stating the essential difference between the 1936 and the 2013 bridges.

Notes

1. Altshuler and Luberoff, *Mega-Projects*.

2. Bent Flyvjberg, Mette K. Skampris Holm, and Soren Buhl, "How Common and How Large Are Cost Overruns in Transport Infrastructure Projects?" *Transport Review* 23, no. 1 (2003).

3. These figures are from Altshuler and Luberoff. The experience of the East Span shows, however, how difficult it is to compare various cost estimates because the project changes quickly. For the East Span project, the most important cost estimate was the estimate used to justify a new bridge versus a retrofit. That estimate was about $1 billion. The fact that the East Span ultimately cost $6.4 billion makes the cost overruns on a percentage basis higher than either the Big Dig or airport in Denver.

4. I use the term *benefit-cost ratio* loosely here, to refer to perceived benefit and real costs. There is an established science of benefit-cost ratio that is itself subject to considerable interpretation.

5. Bent Flyvjberg, Nils Bruzelius, Werner Rothengatter, *Megaprojects and Risk: Anatomy of Ambition* (Cambridge, UK: Cambridge University Press, 2003), 2.

6. Glen Martin, "Bridge Over Troubled Bolts: UC Berkeley Experts Raised Safety Concerns about New Bay Bridge," Cal Alumni Association. October 27, 2013.

7. The benefit-cost ratio of the 2013 Bay Bridge work is analyzed by Karen Trapenberg Frick in "The Cost of the Technological Sublime: Daring Ingenuity and the New San Francisco–Oakland Bay Bridge," in Hugo Priemus, et al. (eds), *Decision-Making on Mega-Projects: Benefit-Cost Analysis, Planning and Innovation* (London, UK: Edward Elgar Publishing, 2008)

8. FHWA, "The Importance of Purpose and Need in Environmental Documents," NEPA and Transportation Decision-making, September 18, 1990, http://www.environment.fhwa.dot.gov/projdev/tdmneed.asp.

9. Perata quoted in "Simpler? Definitely. Cheaper? Maybe," *San Francisco Chronicle*, December 11, 2004.

10. McClintock quoted in Frick, "The Making and Un-Making of the San Francisco–Oakland Bay Bridge," 187.

11. Peralta quoted in "Peralta, Torlakson Offer Bridge Proposal," *San Francisco Chronicle*, April 10, 2005.

12. Flyvjberg, Skampris Holm, and Buhl, "How Common and How Large," 20.

13. Altshuler and Luberoff, *Mega-Projects*, 246.

14. Flyvjberg, Skampris Holm, and Buhl, "How Common and How Large," 20.

15. Wachs quoted in Altshuler and Luberoff, *Mega-Projects*, 246.

16. Ibid., 367.

17. Ibid., 94.

18. http://stran.senate.ca.gov/archivedinformationalhearingmaterials

19. Senate Transportation and Housing Committee, "The San Francisco–Oakland Bay Bridge: Basic Reforms for the Future." January 2014, 4.

20. Steve Poftak, "What Exactly is the MBTA's 'Big Dig Debt'?" Pioneer Institute, Public Policy Research, March 1, 2012, http://pioneerinstitute.org/news/what-exactly-is-the-mbtas-big-dig-debt/

21. Brown quoted in Frick, "The Making and Un-Making of the San Francisco–Oakland Bay Bridge," 18.

22. Moran to Woodruff, November 9, 1931, California State Archives, 200.5. Sacramento, CA.

23. Ibid.

24. Modjeski to Purcell, February 17, 1931, California State Archives, 200.5.

25. Brown in a Letter to the Editor, *Vacaville Reporter*, August 6, 2004.

26. Hess quoted in Frick, "The Making and Un-Making of the San Francisco–Oakland Bay Bridge," 107.

27. King quoted in "New Bay Bridge Span Dazzles as it Takes Shape," *San Francisco Chronicle*, July 13, 2010.

Bibliography

This book relies on primary sources for the history of the two bridges and secondary sources for biographical material and for the history of bridges other than the Bay Bridge.

For the history of the 1936 bridge, the most useful sources are found at the California State Archives in Sacramento, the California State Library in Sacramento, and at the Bancroft Library in Berkeley.

For the history of the still-young 2013 bridge, the library at the Metropolitan Transportation Commission (MTC) in Oakland is the most definitive resource. The MTC has collected all available reports from Caltrans, from the MTC, and from other governmental agencies. It also has an extensive clippings file, geared chiefly toward Bay Area newspapers.

For contextual information, I visited various libraries with a technical orientation, including the Physical Sciences & Engineering Library at the University of California–Davis.

Books

Adler, Seymour. *The Political Economy of Transit in the San Francisco Bay Area*. Berkeley, CA: Institute of Urban and Regional Development, 1980.

Altshuler, Alan, and David Luberoff. *Mega-Projects: The Changing Politics of Urban Public Investment*. Washington, DC: Brookings Institution, 2003.

Anonymous. *Purcell Pontifex: A Tribute*. This book, available at the California State Library, is noted as "Privately Printed by His Friends."

Billington, David P. *The Tower and the Bridge: The New Art of Structural Engineering*. Princeton, NJ: Princeton, 1985.

Bortles, Scott. *Los Angeles and the Automobile: The Making of a Modern City*. Berkeley: University of California Press, 1987.

Brown, Peter Handee. *America's Waterfront Revival: Port Authorities and Urban Redevelopment*. Philadelphia: University of Pennsylvania, 2009.

Dermoro, Harry W. *The Key Route: Transbay Commuting by Train and Ferry*. Glendale, CA: Interurban Press, 1985.

Flick, James L. *The Car Culture*. Cambridge, MA: MIT Press, 1975.

Flyvjberg, Bent, Nils Bruzelius, and Werner Rothengatter. *Megaprojects and Risk: Anatomy of Ambition*. Cambridge, UK: Cambridge University Press, 2003.

Fogelson, Robert M. *The Fragmented Metropolis, Los Angeles, 1850–1930*. Cambridge, MA: Harvard University Press, 1967.

Forsyth, Raymond, and Joseph Hagwood. *One Hundred Years of Progress: A Photographic Essay on the Development of the California Transportation System*. Sacramento, CA: California Transportation Foundation, 1998.

Frick, Karen Trapenberg. "The Cost of the Technological Sublime: Daring Ingenuity and the New San Francisco–Oakland Bay Bridge." In *Decision-Making on Mega-Projects: Benefit-Cost Analysis, Planning and Innovation*, edited by Hugo Priemus, Bent Flyvbjerg, and Bert van Wee. London: Edward Elgar Publishing, 2008.

——. *Remaking the San Francisco–Oakland Bay Bridge: A Case of Shadow-boxing with Nature*. London: Routledge, 2015.

Gerston, Larry, and Terry Christensen. *Recall: California's Political Earthquake*. Armonk, NY: M. E. Sharpe, 2004.

Harlan, George H. *San Francisco Bay Ferryboats*. Berkeley, CA: Howell-North Books, 1967.

Hessen, Robert. *Herbert Hoover and the Bay Bridge: A Commemorative Essay*. Stanford, CA: Hoover Institute, 1986.

Hildebrand, George Herbert. *Borax Pioneer: Francis Marion Smith*. Westwood, NJ: Howell-North Books, 1982.

Issel, William. "New Deal and Wartime Origins of San Francisco's Postwar Political Culture: The Case of Growth Politic and Policy." In *The Way We Really Were: The Golden State in the Second Great War*, edited by Roger W. Lotchin. Champaign: University of Illinois Press, 2000.

Jackson, Donald C. *Great American Bridges and Dams*. Washington, DC: Preservation Press, 1988.

Lotchin, Roger W. *Fortress California: From Warfare to Welfare, 1910–1960*. New York: Oxford University Press, 1992.

MacDonald, Donald, and Ira Nadel. *Bay Bridge: History and Design of a New Icon*. San Francisco, CA: Chronicle Books, 2013.

Mikesell, Stephen D. *Historic Highway Bridges of California*. Sacramento, CA: California Department of Transportation, 1990.

Olson, James Stuart. *Herbert Hoover and the Reconstruction Finance Corporation, 1931–1933*. Ames: Iowa State University Press, 1977.

Petroski, Henry. *Engineers of Dreams: Great Bridge Builders and the Spanning of America*. New York: Random House, 2010.

Rice, Walter Rice, and Emiliano Echeverria. *The Key System: San Francisco and the Eastshore Empire*. Charleston, SC: Arcadia Books, 2007.

Scott, Mel. *The San Francisco Bay Area: A Metropolis in Perspective*. Berkeley: University of California Press, 1985.

Stackpole, Peter. *The Bridge Builders*. Petaluma, CA: Pomegranate Artbooks, 1984.

Starr, Kevin. *Endangered Dreams: The Great Depression in California*. New York: Oxford University Press, 1996.

———. *Golden Gate: The Life and Times of America's Greatest Bridge*. New York: Bloomsbury Press, 2010.

Steinman, David B., and Sara Ruth Watson. *Bridges and Their Builders*. New York: Dover Publications, 1941.

Trimble, Paul C. *Railways of San Francisco*. Charleston, SC: Arcadia Books, 2004.

———. *Interurban Railways of the Bay Area*. Fresno, CA: Valley Publishers, 1977.

Trimble, Paul C., and John C. Alioto Jr. *The Bay Bridge*. Charleston, SC: Arcadia Publishing, 2004.

Van der Zee, John. *The Gate: The True Story of the Design and Construction of the Golden Gate Bridge*. New York: Simon & Schuster, 1986.

Weingardt, Ralph. *Engineering Legends: Great American Civil Engineers*. Reston, VA: American Society of Civil Engineers Publications, 2005.

Articles

Billington, David P. "Historical Perspective on Prestressed Concrete." *PCI Journal* (January–February 2004).

Billington, David P., and Aly Nazmy. "History and Aesthetics of Cable-stayed Bridges." *Journal of Structural Engineering* 107, no. 10 (1993): 3013–34.

Booker, B. W. "Freeways in District IV." *California Highways and Public Works* (March–April, 1957).

"Daniel E. Moran: Memoir." *Transactions ASCE* [American Society of Civil Engineers] (1938): 1840–44.

"Downtown Location Recommended for San Francisco Bay Bridge." *Engineering News–Record* (May 19, 1927): 821.

Elliott, Arthur L. "High Level Engineering." *Civil Engineering* (October 1986).

Flyvjberg, Bent, Mette K. Skampris Holm, and Soren Buhl. "How Common and How Large Are Cost Overruns in Transport Infrastructure Projects?" *Transport Review* 23, no. 1 (2003).

Foley, E. R. "Bay Bridge Reconstruction." *California Highways and Public Works* (March–April 1964).

"Glenn Barton Woodruff, F. ASCE." *Transactions ASCE* [American Society of Civil Engineers] 139 (1974): 5880.

Hess, Alan. "A Bridge to Take Us from Whimsy to Expensive Looniness." *San Jose Mercury News* (April 5, 1998).

Kelly, Earl Lee. "Bridge Mighty Symbol of California Genius and Vision." *California Highway and Public Works* (November 1936).

Proctor, Carlton S. "Foundation Design for the Trans-Bay Bridge." *Civil Engineering* 4, no. 12 (December 1934): 617–21.

Purcell, C. H. "Californian Highway Expenditures as Compared with Other States." *California Highways and Public Works* (March–April 1929).

Purcell, C. H., Charles E. Andrew, and Glenn B. Woodruff. "San Francisco–Oakland Bay Bridge: A Review of the Preliminaries." *Engineering News–Record* (March 22, 1934): 371.

"San Francisco Bay Bridge Projects Total 17." *Engineering News–Record* (October 28, 1926): 720.

Skeggs, Col. John H. "The Modern El Camino Real." *California Highways and Public Works* (May 1930).

——. "The Bayshore Highway Dedication." *California Highways and Public Works* (November 1929).

——. "Important Progress on East Bay Highway." *California Highways and Public Works* (July–August 1930).

Unpublished Dissertations and Other Studies

Frick, Karen Trapenberg. "The Making and Un-Making of the San Francisco–Oakland Bay Bridge: A Case in Megaproject Planning and Decisionmaking." Doctoral dissertation, University of California–Berkeley, Fall 2005.

Van Goolen, David. "Self-Anchored Suspension Bridges." Master of science thesis. Delft University of Technology, Delft, the Netherlands, 2004.

Governmental Reports

Abolhassan Astaneh-Asl. "First Draft of Seismic Retrofit Concepts for the Bay Bridge." Sacramento, CA. 1992.

California Department of Public Works. "First Annual Progress Report, San Francisco–Oakland Bay Bridge." Sacramento, CA. July 1, 1934.

Bartholomew, Harland. "The San Francisco Bay Region: A Statement Concerning the Nature and Importance of a Plan for Future Growth." San Francisco, CA. 1925.

Bureau of State Audits (BSA). "Caltrans Employees Engaged in Inexcusable Neglect of Duty, Received Overpayment for Overtime, Falsified Test Data, and Misappropriated State Property." Report 2009-0640. Sacramento, CA. 2009.

California Department of Transportation (Caltrans). "Seismic Retrofit of the San Francisco–Oakland Bay Bridge: Report to the California Transportation Commission." Sacramento, CA. September 10, 1992.

——. *San Francisco–Oakland Bay Bridge Seismic Safety Project, Replacement vs. Retrofit.* Sacramento, CA. April 2000.

———. *Cost Estimate Investigation for a Replacement Structure for the East Spans of the San Francisco–Oakland Bay Bridge*. Office of Structure Design, California Department of Transportation (Caltrans), Sacramento, CA. September 1996.

California Legislative Affairs Office. "Hard Decisions before the Legislature: Toll Bridge Seismic Retrofit." Sacramento, CA. January 24, 2005.

California State Senate Transportation Committee. "Department of Transportation: Bridge Foundation Inspection Practices." Sacramento, CA. November 22, 2011.

Department of California Highway Patrol. "1989 Loma Prieta Earthquake Summary Report." Sacramento, CA. 1989.

Dunphy, Dean. "Memorandum to Governor Pete Wilson: Consideration of Replacement of the Eastern Spans of the San Francisco–Oakland Bay Bridge." Sacramento, CA. January 10, 1997.

Endersby, V. A. "Final Construction Report of the Substructure, East Bay Crossing, San Francisco–Oakland Bay Bridge Contracts 4 and 4a." Sacramento, CA. July 28, 1937.

Federal Highway Administration. "Value Engineering Final Rule," Federal Highway Administration, U.S. Department of Transportation, Washington, DC. https://www.fhwa.dot.gov/ve/

Governor's Board of Inquiry on the 1989 Loma Prieta Earthquake. "Competing Against Time." Sacramento, CA. May 1990.

Hoover–Young San Francisco Bay Bridge Commission Report (*Hoover–Young Report*). "Report to the President of the United States and the Governor of California." San Francisco, CA. August 1930.

Jahlstrom, I. O. "General Construction Report for Foundations, Piers 2, 3, 4, 5, 6 and 24 of Contract No. 2 for the West Bay Crossing of the San Francisco–Oakland Bay Bridge." Sacramento, CA. February 27, 1937.

Maroney, Brian, and Caltrans. *Replacement Study for the East Spans of the San Francisco–Oakland Bay Bridge Seismic Safety Project*. Sacramento, CA. December 17, 1996.

Nelson, John, Stephen D. Mikesell, Dan Peterson, and Mark Ketchum. *San Francisco–Oakland Bay Bridge*. HAER No. CA-32. San Francisco: Historic American Engineering Record, 1999. [Historical background by Stephen D. Mikesell, photography by John Nelson, architectural and engineering drawings by San Peterson and Mark Ketchum.]

National Institute of Standards and Technology (NIST). Special Publication 778. "Performance of Structures during the Loma Prieta Earthquake of October 17, 1989." Washington, DC. January 1990.

Pavetti, C. V. "History of Highway Financing and Allocation Process in California." Highway Planning and Research Branch, California Department of Transportation (Caltrans). Sacramento, CA. 1983.

Ridgway, Robert, Arthur N. Talbot, and John Galloway. "Report of the Board of Engineers, Transbay Bridge, San Francisco, May 1927." San Francisco, CA.

Ventry Engineering, the National Constructor's Group, Tokola Corporation, and OPAC Consulting Engineers. *San Francisco–Oakland Bay Bridge, East Bay Crossing Replacement Value Analysis Findings*, Sacramento, CA. December 1996.

Archives

The California State Archives retains the records of the Bay Bridge Division, hundreds of folders that include correspondence between and among the designers of the Bay Bridge.

The Bancroft Library in Berkeley retains hundreds of photographs showing the construction of the Bay Bridge in 1936.

The California Department of Transportation (Caltrans) retains the original plans for the 1936 bridge, in linen and in copies. The Caltrans History Library in Sacramento also contains oral histories of many engineers who worked on the Bay Bridge.

The Historic American Engineering Record includes photographs and written histories of many great bridges, including the Bay Bridge.

About the Author

Stephen Mikesell is a historic preservation specialist and public historian, and lives in Davis, California. He has worked in the historic preservation field since 1980, including a decade serving as the deputy state historic preservation officer in California. He has also worked for private environmental consulting firms, ranging from small businesses to a NASDAQ-traded corporation. He currently runs Mikesell Historical Consulting, a small historic preservation consulting firm in Davis.

Throughout his career Mr. Mikesell has focused on preserving and documenting historic bridges and other engineering resources. His professional work has involved historic engineering features in California, Nevada, Oregon, and Washington. He has appeared in speaking parts on documentary films on historic bridges, including a film on the Los Angeles River bridges and a film on the career of Ralph Modjeski, the principal engineer for the San Francisco–Oakland Bay Bridge.

He has written extensively, including *Historic Highway Bridges of California* (1990) and historic bridge–related articles in *The Public Historian* and *Southern California Quarterly*. He wrote a book on the steam-era rail line, *The Sierra Railway* (2016). His interest in the San Francisco–Oakland Bay Bridge dates to 1998, when he wrote the historical documentation for the Historic American Engineering Record, prior to demolition of the East Span of the bridge. Mr. Mikesell holds a bachelor's degree in history from Harvard University and a master's degree in history from the University of California–Davis. He is married with two grown children.

Index